I0079641

# I'VE SEEN THE PROMISED LAND

*Martin Luther King, Jr.
and the 21st Century Quest
for the Beloved Community*

## C. Anthony Hunt

# I've Seen The Promised Land

*Martin Luther King, Jr. and the 21<sup>st</sup> Century Quest
for the Beloved Community*

by C. Anthony Hunt

***The Rhodes-Fulbright Library series***

**ALL RIGHTS RESERVED.**

No part of this book may be reproduced, stored in a retrieval system, or transmitted by any form or by any means, electronic, mechanical, photocopying, recording, or otherwise, except as may be expressly permitted by the applicable copyright statutes or in writing by the publisher or the author.

ISBN: 978-1-55605-477-8
Ebook: 978-1-55605-478-5


Cover Design by: Kristen E. Hunt

WYNDHAM HALL PRESS
Levering, MI 49755
www.wyndhamhallpress.com

Printed in The United States of America

# CONTENTS

*CHAPTER ONE*

*REV. DR. MARTIN LUTHER KING, JR. AND A
LETTER TO AMERICA (JANUARY 15, 2019)................10*

*CHAPTER TWO*

*THE ROOTS OF RESISTANCE:*

*MARTIN LUTHER KING, JR.'S SPIRITUAL, SOCIAL
AND INTELLECTUAL DEVELOPMENT.......................14*

*CHAPTER THREE*

*SOUL FORCE - MOHANDAS GANDHI, MARTIN
LUTHER KING, JR. AND THE POWER OF LOVE.......46*

*CHAPTER FOUR*

*I'VE BEEN TO THE MOUNTAINTOP –*

*THE PROPHETIC LIFE AND LEGACY OF MARTIN
LUTHER KING, JR.................................................86*

*CHAPTER FIVE*

*THEOLOGICAL AND SOCIOLOGICAL DIMENSIONS
OF THE BELOVED COMMUNITY..............................117*

*CHAPTER SIX*

*MARTIN LUTHER KING, JR. THE CHRISTIAN LOVE-
ETHIC AND NONVIOLENCE*............................................*136*


*CHAPTER SEVEN*

*OUT OF THE MOUNTAIN OF DESPAIR – MARTIN
LUTHER KING, JR. AND HOPE*...................................*157*


*CHAPTER EIGHT*

*I'VE SEEN THE PROMISED LAND -    MARTIN
LUTHER KING, JR. AND THE  21st CENTURY QUEST
FOR THE BELOVED COMMUNITY*............................*172*


*ENDNOTES*.................................................................*218*

**About The Author** ...................................................**277**

## INTRODUCTION

Rev. Dr. Martin Luther King, Jr.'s singular vision was for the realization of the *Beloved Community*. In their seminal 1974 work entitled, *Search for the Beloved Community*, Kenneth Smith and Ira Zepp, Jr. suggested that King's perspective on the Christian love-ethic provides critical insight into understanding his persistent search for the *Beloved Community*. For him, it was rooted in the biblical notion of *agape* (God's unconditional love), and was the ultimate goal for society.[1] When characterizing King's conception of the *Beloved Community*, Smith and Zepp wrote that King saw it "as a transformed and regenerated human society".[2] Walter E. Fluker in *They Looked for a City* asserts that in King's thinking, the beloved community was synonymous with the Kingdom of God.[3]

My first awareness of the significance of Martin Luther King, Jr. came when I was seven years old. Although, I had heard about him from my parents and grandparents, and his name had been mentioned by teachers in the two elementary schools I had attended up to that point, I was not fully aware of who King was, and his significance until April 4, 1968. That was the day he was assassinated in Memphis, Tennessee. I was born in Washington, DC in 1961. The 1960s was a time when – although I did not really realize it until I was a teenager – the Nation's Capital was effectively a city segregated by sectors. I grew up in the southeastern quadrant of the District of Columbia in a section called Anacostia. Any persons who have grown up in DC, lived there for any period of time, or visited and stayed for any length of time have come to realize that "Anacostia" in many ways is a euphemism for what it means to live east of the Anacostia River.

The Anacostia River effectively divides Washington, DC into eastern and western sectors, and the river has historically divided the city in more general, yet pronounced, ways along lines of what it means to grow up relatively poorer or richer – which is generally evident in the quality of schools/education, hospitals/healthcare, policing/safety, roads, transportation, food/nutrition, stores, housing, and so on. In many ways, to borrow a theme from Charles Dickens' great 19th century novel, this speaks to *the tale of two cities.*

Over time, I came to realize that to have been reared in Anacostia carried with it a number of assumptions about who one might become, and the length and breadth of one's likely social mobility and success in life. To be from Anacostia effectively meant that one was reared in a socially and physically segregated space which, at the time of my upbringing, was well over 85 percent Black, and largely populated by poor, working-class, and at-most barely middle-class persons.

Over time, I also came to realize that the realities and images of segregation were exacerbated in my community in Anacostia, and others in DC and across the nation at Martin Luther King, Jr.'s assassination on April 4, 1968 at 6:01 p.m. on the balcony of the Lorraine Motel in Memphis. As riots and unrest erupted throughout DC and in cities across the nation, it seemed that our Southeast DC neighborhood had been invaded by those – the National Guard – most of whose members did not look like us (they were white and we were black). We wondered whether the National Guard had been sent to Anacostia to protect us, or to fence us in and thus protect those in other neighborhoods outside ours from us. In any event, the riots and social unrest in DC and across the nation in April 1968 spoke to the seminal contributions that King had made in changing America, and raising the nation's conscience as it regards racial, class and social injustice. These events also spoke to the deep disappointment and pain among many persons across the nation and world at King's untimely assassination at the young age of 39, and the sense that with his death, his dream for America had, in no small ways, died with him.

King's significance and impact on my life continued to grow through my high school years. I realize now that in every year of junior and senior high school, my choice of subjects/topics for every book report and research paper that I worked on were Rev. Dr. Martin Luther King, Jr. and the American Civil Rights movement. This pattern of intellectual curiosity continued through college and graduate school. I now also realize that I was actually beginning to write my doctor of philosophy dissertation while I was in junior high school in the mid-1970s, which became a comparative analysis of the thought and theology of Howard Thurman, Martin Luther King, Jr., and Peacemaking, which I completed and defended on September 10, 2001, and which would be published in 2005 as *Blessed are the Peacemakers: A Theological Analysis of the Thought of Howard Thurman and Martin Luther King, Jr.*

This current volume, *I've Seen the Promised Land*, will examine Martin Luther King, Jr.'s life, ministry and writings in light of an overarching concern with how his vision of the *Beloved Community* might be conceived, articulated and appropriated for the church and society today and into the future. It is proposed that King's ecclesiology and moral philosophy - and specifically the quest for the *Beloved Community* - were foundational to his overall theological project, and ultimately served as the framework for his conception of humanity, the ministry and mission of the Christian church, and hope for the world.

One always writes within the context of experience and community, and thus I am indebted to many in my community who continue to help shape my thinking, strengthen my faith, and who have been instrumental in all that's written in this volume. I am grateful for my family – my wife Lisa, and our children Marcus (deceased), Kristen and Brian. I am also thankful for my parents, the late William Delaney and Amelia Mae Hunt who taught and modeled the ways of the *Beloved Community*. I dedicate this volume to my wife, Lisa who has been a co-laborer with me as a companion, parent, confidante, encourager and best friend, and who has supported my work as a pastor, religious scholar and community leader for over three decades. Without her, I would not be.

The faith community that I have been privileged to serve and lead as pastor since 2011, Epworth Chapel United Methodist Church in Baltimore, Maryland has also been instrumental in helping to shape this volume. Daily, we are a congregation that seeks to become the *Beloved Community* that God calls us to be. For the places where I am privileged to teach - St. Mary's Seminary and University (Baltimore, MD), Wesley Theological Seminary (Washington, DC), the Graduate Theological Foundation (Oklahoma City, OK), and United Theological Seminary (Dayton, OH) – I am forever appreciative of the lessons that I've learned, taught and written about community, and continue to learn. To Kristen Hunt, who is responsible for the cover design for this volume, I am also grateful.

My prayer is that this volume will serve as a testament to the life and seminal contributions of Rev. Dr. Martin Luther King, Jr., and speak to our collective hopes and strivings as we endeavor to be the *Beloved Community* in the days ahead.

## CHAPTER ONE

## REV. DR. MARTIN LUTHER KING, JR. AND A LETTER TO AMERICA (JANUARY 15, 2019)

This year (2019) marks the 90th anniversary of Rev. Dr. Martin Luther King, Jr.'s birth, and the 51$^{st}$ year after his assassination on April 4, 1968 in Memphis, Tennessee. As was the case in 1968, the nation and world today are fraught with social, economic, political and religious upheaval. Over the past several years, in the United States and across the globe, we have become more divided along various lines. In the U.S., the social and political division that we now experience is not really new, but it challenges our sense of normalcy in ways that it perhaps has not been challenged in the past.

In April of 1963, King wrote a letter to eight clergymen in Birmingham, Alabama which has come to be known as his Letter from Birmingham Jail, and on August 28th of the same year in Washington, DC, at the urging of gospel singer Mahalia Jackson, who encouraged him to "Tell them about the Dream Martin!", King delivered the concluding recitation in what has come to be known as his "I Have a Dream" speech.

In the Birmingham letter and Washington, DC speech, King demonstratively outlined his singular vision for the realization of the *Beloved Community*. His assessment in the Letter from Birmingham Jail was that many churches and their leaders had been found wanting in the sphere of prophetic witness, and had too often remained complicit in their silence and complacent in their inaction with regard to the need to address racial, social and economic oppression. He stated in the letter that "The church must be reminded that it is not the master or the servant of the state, but rather the conscience of the state. It must be the guide and the critic of the state." King further stated that, "There comes a time when silence becomes betrayal." In the "I Have a Dream" speech, he essentially described to the world his dream of the *Beloved Community*, when girls and boys of all races could play together and go to school together, and where people would be judged by the content of their character, and not the color of their skin.

And so today, we might wonder what King would say if he were alive to write a letter to America. Here might be his letter to America in 2019:

*Dear My American Sisters and Brothers,*

*I greet you in the agapic love of Christ, our Savior. I pray that all of you who now dwell in what is deemed to be the land of the free and the home of the brave find yourselves reasonably well. In looking back over the more than 50 years since my last public address at Mason Temple Church of God in Christ, in Memphis, Tennessee on the night of April 3, 1968, and my assassination on a balcony at the Lorraine Motel at 6:01 p.m. the following evening in that same city, much has occurred in America.*

*Much of the progress that was eventuated up to my death, as seen in the passing of national Civil Rights legislation in 1964, and Voting Rights legislation in 1965 seemed to come to full fruition with the election of Barack H. Obama in 2008 as the 44ᵗʰ President of the United States, the first African American to hold the nation's highest office. And yet, subsequent years have seen the heightened emergence (or re-emergence) of evils such as racism, classism, sexism and misogyny, homophobia, war and terror that have served to perpetuate and exacerbate division in much of society, and even in large segments of the churches. I remind you of what I deemed to be the "triplets of evil" – racism, classism/poverty and war – and that these, in many ways, continue to encumber America's progress as a nation.*

*In light of the challenges that confront you, I remind you to remain cognizant that, as I also shared during my life, there is a certain collective force among those of you who are committed to living the sentiments of the prophet Micah to "love kindness, do justice and walk humbly with God" (Micah 6:8). As I stated, "For when people get caught up with that which is right, and they are willing to sacrifice for it, there is no stopping point short of victory."*

*America, in light of all that now fractures you, like immigration at your borders and violence on many of your city's streets, I want to also remind you of how each of you has been created. The nature of humanity is that you have all been created by the same God, and God loves all of that which has been divinely created. Therefore, I remind you of the inherent worth, dignity and "somebodiness" in each of you. As I shared years ago, "all life is interrelated." All of life is part of a single process; all living things are interconnected; and all of you are sisters and brothers. Because all of you are interrelated, you cannot harm another person without harming yourself.*

*There is a great deal more that I could share, but I will conclude my letter by encouraging you to never give up hoping. Regarding hope, I remind you of my past sentiments that "hope is the refusal to give up despite overwhelming odds", and that hope is "animated and undergirded by faith and love." Remember, if you have hope, you have faith in something.*

*Never forget my words on the steps of the Lincoln Memorial in August 1963 in the dream that I shared with the nation on that day that there would someday be "[hewn] out of the mountain of despair, a stone of hope."*

*My dream for you, America, remains the same as it was almost 56 years ago, that the Beloved Community will become a reality. As always, I pray that your best days and most blessed days are not behind you, but in your future.*

*With Agapic Love,*
*Your Brother Martin*

## CHAPTER TWO

## THE ROOTS OF RESISTANCE: MARTIN LUTHER KING, JR.'S SPIRITUAL, SOCIAL AND INTELLECTUAL DEVELOPMENT

In order to comprehensively understand Martin Luther King, Jr.'s public achievements - it is critical to consider the spiritual, social and intellectual influences on his life. Throughout his public life, he consistently reached down into the deep streams of the religious experience and social integration that had been so integral to his early formation. It was within these streams that he consistently discovered and re-discovered the essence of his faith in God, which would ultimately sustain him in his constant beckoning for persons in the church and society to heed the words of the prophet Amos, to:

*"Let justice roll down as waters, and righteousness as an ever-flowing stream"* (Amos 5:24).

And the prophet Micah to:

*"love kindness, do justice, and walk humbly with God"* (Micah 6:8).

Any examination of King's public intellectual life must be understood within the context of the faith that he lived, the lessons of theology and fellowship that he taught, and the hope of the *Beloved Community* that he perpetually sought to convey to the whole of humanity. In many of the biographical works that have been written on King, a great deal of attention has been given to his intellectual development at Morehouse College in Atlanta, GA, Crozer Theological Seminary near Chester, PA and Boston University where he completed his doctoral studies in 1955. Certainly, his intellectual development at these institutions, along with additional academic work at Harvard University and the University of Pennsylvania, provided much of the intellectual foundation for his public ministry. These institutions provided a great amount of the "fertile ground" necessary for progress in what he would refer to as "a serious intellectual quest for a method to eliminate social evil."

But Lewis V. Baldwin, in *There is A Balm: The Cultural Roots of Martin Luther King, Jr.,* intimates that in order to fully comprehend King's movement towards a theological praxis of nonviolent social resistance and direct action as a prophetic preacher, public theologian and civil rights leader, his experiences and development at these institutions must be considered against the backdrop, and within the context of his earlier development – in his family, church and the larger black community.[4]

## I. Early Spiritual Development

There were essentially three major overarching influences extant in King's early life that shaped his later attitudes, thoughts and behaviors. These were: (1) his black middle-class family (which included his extended family) and the family/community ethos in which he was raised; (2) the religious ethos and *mores* of the southern black Baptist church; and (3) the ongoing patterns of racial segregation and discrimination in the South.

Baldwin suggests that King's cultural roots were "folk, black, and southern."[5] These cultural roots remained a part of his thought and praxis through his adult years. Foundational to his early development were his family experiences. Robert Franklin, in *Liberating Visions,* suggests that King's fundamental character was shaped and nurtured within the valuing context of the southern middle-class Black family structure.[6] The Kings and Williamses were prominent leaders in the "new South." His family tree included a long line of Baptist preachers (his father, grandfather and great-grandfather were ministers), and outspoken advocates for freedom and justice.

King's father and grandfather were not only Baptist ministers, but also pioneering exponents of a distinctively African-American version of social gospel Christianity. When his grandfather, the Reverend A. D. Williams, arrived in Atlanta in 1893, social gospel activism was becoming increasingly common among both black and white urban clergypersons. After taking over the pastorate of Atlanta's Ebenezer Baptist Church in March 1894, Williams built a large congregation through forceful preaching that addressed the everyday concerns of poor and working-class residents. Baptist denominational practices encouraged ministers such as Williams to retain the support of occasionally rebellious congregations through charismatic leadership that extended beyond purely spiritual matters.   Having arrived in Atlanta on the eve of a major period of institutional development among African-American Baptists, Williams joined two thousand other delegates and visitors who met at Atlanta's Friendship Baptist Church in September 1895 to organize the National Baptist Convention, the largest black religious organization in the United States.[7]

When Martin Luther King, Jr. was very young, his parents noticed that M.L. (as he was affectionately known) possessed an unusual ability to endure pain.   Although obviously in pain during spankings, M.L. refused to cry. Franklin suggests that this ability to endure pain would become evident again, as King would later face the (emotional and physical) injury of American racism.[8]

King's later views on and activism against racism in America are clearly traced to his early development.   In his biography on King, *Let the Trumpet Sound*, Stephen B. Oates reports on King's preschool years, when his closest playmate was a white boy whose father owned the store across the street from the King family home.   When the two friends entered school in 1935, they attended separate schools.   One day, the parents of his friend announced that M.L. could no longer play with their son.   Their explanation was, "Because we are white and you are colored."[9]

Later, around the dinner table, King's parents responded to his hurt by telling him the story of the black experience in America.   It was typically through conversations such as this (around the dinner table) that black youth would be socialized into the protest traditions of the black community and church.[10]

King's early childhood experiences with racism predisposed him to study and address the psychological and social effects of race and class oppression. His later formal education was predicated upon and guided by the more informal learning and personal experiences of his early years within the nurturing context of a close-knit family, church and community.

Benefiting from extensive exposure to African-American family, church and community structures, King then was able to perceive theological training as a means of reconciling his inclination to follow in his father's ministerial path with his desire for intellectual acceptability. His descriptions of his decision to enter the ministry reveal that he had accepted the social mission of the church even though he had not yet resolved his theological doubts. He realized that the Baptist religion he had absorbed during his youth had derived mainly from daily contact with church life rather than from theological reflection, and the typical conversion experience and personal encounter with God. Growing up in the church provided a substitute for orthodox theological convictions; born a Baptist, he never felt the need to affirm all the tenets of the denomination. In his 1950 essay "An Autobiography of Religious Development," King explained: "Conversion for me was never an abrupt something. I have never experienced the so-called 'crisis moment.' Religion has just been something I grew up in. Conversion for me has been a gradual intaking of the noble ideals set forth in my family and my environment, and I must admit that this intaking has been largely unconscious."[11]

Although his published descriptions of his "pilgrimage to nonviolence" generally emphasized the impact of his academic training, he also was careful to acknowledge his black Baptist roots. "I am many things to many people," he acknowledged in 1965, "but in the quiet recesses of my heart, I am fundamentally a clergyman, a Baptist preacher. This is my being and my heritage, for I am also the son of a Baptist preacher, the grandson of a Baptist preacher, and the great-grandson of a Baptist preacher."[12]

## *II. Intellectual Development*

Martin Luther King, Jr.'s intellectual formation can be understood within the context of his earlier development. Clayborne Carson asserts that King was deeply influenced by his childhood immersion in African-American religious life, but his years at Crozer Seminary and Boston University increased his ability to incorporate aspects of academic theology into sermons and public speeches.[13] His student papers demonstrate that he adopted European-American ideological ideas that ultimately reinforced, rather than undermined the African-American social gospel tradition embraced by his father and grandfather. Although his advanced theological training set him apart from most African-American clergypersons of his day, the documentary evidence regarding his formative years suggests that his graduate studies engendered an increased appreciation for his African-American religious roots.

From childhood, King had been exposed to, but was uncomfortable with the emotionalism and scriptural literalism that he associated with traditional Baptist praxis, but he was also familiar with innovative, politically active, and intellectually sophisticated African-American clergymen who had themselves been influenced by European-American theological scholarship. These clergymen served as role models for King as he mined theological scholarship for nuggets of insight that could enrich his preaching and ministerial praxis. As he sought to resolve religious doubts that had initially prevented him from accepting his ministerial calling, he looked upon European-American theological ideas not as alternatives to traditional black Baptist beliefs, but as necessary correctives to those beliefs.[14]

Although King had been reared in the fundamentalist, relatively simplistic piety of the black Baptist Protestantism of the South, a fact that almost dissuaded him from entering Christian ministry, he was introduced in his undergraduate studies at Morehouse College and later in his graduate studies at Crozer Seminary to theological liberalism. In a speech before the American Baptist Convention, shortly after the Montgomery Bus Boycott had ended in December 1956, he publicly stated:

> I gained my major influences from...Morehouse and Crozer – and I feel greatly indebted to them. They gave me the basic truths I now believe...the worldview which... I have... the idea of the oneness of humanity, and the dignity and worth of all human

personality... At Crozer I found the actual living out of Christian beliefs.[15]

Carson further posits that King's ongoing intellectual development should be viewed within the context of his struggle to synthesize his father's Christian practices and his own theological skepticism. Seen from this perspective, his experiences at Crozer Seminary and Boston University constituted neither a pilgrimage towards the social gospel views of his Crozer professors, nor a movement towards the personalism of those at Boston. Instead, he eclectically drew upon the writings of academic theologians, and moved away from Christian liberalism towards a theological synthesis closer to aspects of his father's religious faith, and particularly towards a conception of God as a source of support in times of personal need. Rather than becoming more liberal in college and seminary, he became increasingly skeptical of intellectualized, liberalized conceptions of divinity. As he became increasingly aware of the limitations of liberal Christian thought, he acquired a renewed appreciation for his southern Baptist roots.[16]

King's intellectual development is specifically evident in his attraction to: (1) a model of the rational, black minister as organic intellectual as epitomized by Benjamin Elijah Mays at Morehouse College and Mordecai Johnson at Howard University; (2) the evangelical liberalism of George Washington Davis; (3) the philosophy of Personalism of L. Harold DeWolf and Edgar Sheffield Brightman at Boston University; (4) the Christian Liberalism and Social Gospel of Walter Rauschenbusch; (5) the Christian Realism of

Reinhold Niebuhr; and (6) the model of nonviolent, social transformation of Mohandas K. Gandhi. The first five of these streams of intellectual influence will be discussed in this chapter, with a complete analysis of Mohandas Gandhi - his philosophy and influence upon King – provided in Chapter Three.

### A. *Benjamin Elijah Mays*

Upon entering Morehouse College in 1944 at the age of fifteen, Martin Luther King, Jr. was profoundly impressed by the example of the college's president, Benjamin Elijah Mays, a family friend who was the kind of dedicated, intellectually sophisticated religious leader that King wished to emulate. Selected in 1940 to succeed John Hope as head of Morehouse and serving until 1967, Mays was the first Morehouse president with a Ph.D. (University of Chicago). Although not a graduate of Morehouse himself, he had internalized the Morehouse tradition calling for students to use their skills on behalf of the black community.[17]

Mays had previously served as the first dean of the School of Religion at Howard University in Washington, DC from 1934-40, and was considered to be a major Black public intellectual, and the leading African-American theologian of the post-World War II period. Before King's rise to international prominence in the wake of the 1955-56 Montgomery Bus Boycott, Mays was the most assertive public spokesman for the theology of race relations and nonviolence in America; his active participation in ecumenical conferences around the world made him one of the most visible Negro churchmen of his time.[18] As Keith D. Miller notes in his study of King's language and its sources, "What Mays had been to liberal black (and to a lesser degree white) religious and academic circles, King – with the benefit of a huge political movement and television – would be to America."[19]

In his article, "The Christian Way in Race Relations: Benjamin E. Mays and the Theology of Race Relations," Mark L. Chapman points to the significant impact that Mays had on the thinking of King. Mays focused a great deal of his work on seeking to bring comprehension to the race problem in America. This focus is reflected in his 1954 comment:

> We are what we do and not what we say. We are as democratic as we live and we are as Christian as we act. If we talk brotherhood and segregate human beings, we do not believe in brotherhood. If we talk democracy and deny it to certain groups, we do not believe in democracy. If we preach justice and exploit the weak, we do not believe in justice. If we preach truth and tell lies, we do not believe in truth. We are what we do.[20]

Regarding Christianity as a means of addressing the race problem, Mays was quoted again in 1957:

> It is not enough for us to call upon members of different races to be decent toward one another for

the sake of humanity, science or democracy. The basis for good relations is found in Christian religion, in the proper understanding of the Christian doctrine of man, Christ, and God, and in the application of Christian insights and convictions in everyday living.[21]

King's attraction to Mays and other African-American intellectuals and ministers like Mordecai Johnson, president of Howard University from 1926-60, was impacted by the early influence of King's father, grandfather and great-grandfather who, as previously stated, were, before him, also Baptist ministers. This model of ministry and intellectual engagement as practiced by the likes of Mays, is rooted in the notion of what Antonio Gramsci, Cornel West and others have referred to as the "organic intellectual."[22]  In contrast to traditional western models of intellectual life where one's intellectual identity and development typically remain connected to academic institutions as a primary source - the "organic intellectual" remains primarily connected to priestly and communal institutions like the church, other public institutions and the broader community.

King's intellectual life is thus to be viewed in this organic, public dimension as exemplified by his ongoing connection with the Black Baptist church, and later to public institutions such as the Southern Christian Leadership Conference, which he helped to found in 1957.

## B.  George Washington Davis

George Washington Davis, Martin Luther King, Jr.'s professor of Christian Theology at Crozer Seminary, was known as one of the major proponents of evangelical liberalism. Davis was a dynamic embodiment of evangelical liberalism at its very best. Kenneth Smith and Ira Zepp, Jr., assert that King very clearly found some of the answers he had been searching for in the courses that he took from Davis. [23]

The degree of Davis' attachment to evangelical liberalism is evident in the textbooks he used in his courses: William Newton Clarke's *An Outline of Christian Theology* and William Adam Brown's *Christian Theology in Outline*. Davis' methodology and content paralleled the texts very closely. The Clarke and Brown volumes were classical texts in the liberal Christian tradition; both authors had served as theological mentors to a whole generation of liberals like Davis.[24]

In an article published in *Theology Today* in 1948, Davis identified several cardinal tenets of evangelical liberalism. They are summarized as follows:

(1) *The existence of a moral order in the universe (cosmos)* - For Davis, God has a purpose for the human race, and history moves towards a moral goal. Progress towards that goal may appear to be slow, but the outcome is certain; for there is a moral order "which is relevant to the corporate life of men and the ordering of human society." If mankind is to escape

chaos and recurrent war, social and political institutions must be brought into conformity with the moral order.[25]

(2) *The activity of God in history* – Religious humankind, Davis asserted, has always affirmed that there is a divine purpose in history, and the evidence proves that this is a rational belief.

(3) *The value of the personal* – For Davis, a high priority is assigned to the value of personality in Christian faith. Davis linked his belief in the value of the personal with Jesus of Nazareth's emphasis upon the ethic of love. In Jesus of Nazareth we perceive the divine in the human and the intention of God for human life. God's love for humanity was revealed in the life and death of Jesus, and Jesus' sacrifice on the cross attested to the fact that every person is a being of infinite worth. The greatness of Christianity lies in its faith that the proper category of understanding the nature of ultimate reality is personality.

(4) *The social character of human existence* – According to Davis, human existence is fundamentally social in character and human solidarity is the goal towards which history evolves. People are essentially social animals, and it is only within the context of fellowship and cooperation that an individual's character can evolve the way God intends. It is much more likely to grow in democratic, cooperative and Christian societies where people are constantly exhorted to manifest regard for the personal rights and opportunities of others.[26]

(5) *The ethical nature of Christian faith* – For Davis, Christianity is essentially a moral and ethical religion. The goal and test of the Christian faith are its ethical fruits. Davis was concerned throughout his thought to balance the traditional supernatural interpretation of salvation with the ethical interpretation because he felt that the latter had been overshadowed by the former. He approached this subject by observing that Jesus "makes the goal of human character likeness in moral quality to God himself."[27]

Many of the major theological themes that King embraced were rooted in evangelical liberalism as taught by Davis. Davis' stress upon the parenthood of God and the unity of humankind, the centrality of religious experience, the concern of God for all life, the rights of humankind and moral feeling, the humanity of Jesus and his emphasis upon love, the dynamic nature of history and God's action therein, his essential optimism about human nature and history, the tolerance and openness of the liberal spirit, his tolerance towards a pluralism of world religions – all of these were key themes of evangelical liberalism embraced quite early in King's intellectual pilgrimage. Davis, representing the distillation of liberal thought and the irenic spirit of the liberal mind, introduced King to the major motifs that would become integral to his mature thought. King would continue to develop, criticize and synthesize these themes, but he found them first in clearly articulated form in the evangelical liberalism of George Washington Davis.[28]

Specifically, King's later nuanced conception of personalism can be understood in light of George Davis's notion of the value of the personal. King defined personalism as "...the theory that the clue to the meaning of ultimate reality is found in personality. This personal idealism remains today my basic philosophical position."[29] It seems apparent that when Davis claimed, "We know now that we must live together or perish. If we will not have one world, we may have no world" – he presages one of King's main themes, his oft-quoted statement that "the choice of humankind is not between violence and nonviolence, but between nonviolence and nonexistence."[30]

When a person becomes like God in his or her ethical orientation (i.e. exhibits the qualities of love and forgiveness), she or he becomes a child of God. Jesus' words, Davis argued, are explicit: "Love your enemies...that you may be sons." The Christian's ineradicable interest in the good life for all human beings stems from the ethical nature of the Christian faith and the moral foundation of Christian salvation. This theme is explicit in King's emphasis upon the Sermon the Mount as the ethical and spiritual model for Christian behavior.

### C. *Edgar Sheffield Brightman and L. Harold DeWolf*

Martin Luther King, Jr.'s attraction to the personalism of L. Harold DeWolf and Edgar Sheffield Brightman can be viewed within the context of King's consistent striving to develop approaches for understanding humanity and for framing human relations with each other, with the world of nature, and with God. He was introduced to the thinking of Brightman and DeWolf while studying with George W. Davis at Crozer Seminary.

In her autobiography, *My Life with Martin Luther King, Jr.*, Coretta Scott King explained that King chose Boston University as the institution where he would pursue his doctoral degree because he wanted to study the philosophy of personalism with L. Harold DeWolf and Edgar S. Brightman.[31] Gary Dorrien, *in Breaking White Supremacy: Martin Luther King, Jr. and the Black Social Gospel*, points out that on personalism, King's doctoral advisor Harold DeWolf was his chief mentor, although King knew much about personalism before he met DeWolf.[32] This school of thought provided the broad horizon for King's theological, philosophical, pastoral and political orientation.

Personalism is founded on the doctrine of the sanctity and inviolability of the person. According to one of the founders of the school, Ralph Flewelling, in religious terms, personalism is theistic, holding that "the more a person can reach the highest selfhood, the greater his harmony with the Divine nature.[33] Because it is known as the "philosophy of freedom," from a political perspective, it holds that society should be organized so as to "provide the best possible opportunity for the self-development of every human being, as the basis of all true democracy."[34] Brightman defined *Personalism* as a "system of philosophy that regards the universe as an interacting system of persons (or selves)." Everything that exists is either a person or some experience, process, or aspect of a person or persons in relation to each other. All of reality is social or interpersonal. Consequently, "a person is taken to be a complex unity of thought and ideal values."[35]

Rufus Burrow, in *Personalism: A Critical Introduction,* posits that personalists find in the self the clue to the nature of the world and reality. But it is important to remember that the self is not a mirror of the world. That is, we do not find in the self a perfect one-to-one correspondence between our thoughts and ruminations about reality. Our thoughts about God, for example, are neither identical with God, nor are they God.[36]

According to Burrow, one of the reasons that King was attracted to the personalism of Edgar S. Brightman was because of its acknowledgement of the importance of both nonintellectual sources – one's own experiences – and the experiences of one's group. In this regard personalism was much influenced by the Hegelian dictum: "The true is the whole." Therefore, family, church, and black cultural contributions are important in any serious study on King as a person of ideas.[37] Burrow further asserts that unfortunately, King himself did not always place enough emphasis on the nonintellectual sources of his thought when he wrote autobiographical accounts of his life, nor did most early King biographers. As a thoroughgoing personalist who was invested in personalistic methodology, however, King knew that informal and nonintellectual sources and experiences were important in the quest for knowledge and truth.[38]

King's reading of Brightman led him to discover his own spirituality and sense of being:

> How I now long for that religious experience which Dr. Brightman so cogently speaks of through his book. It seems to be an experience, the lack of which life becomes dull and meaningless. As I reflect on the matter, however, I do remember moments that I have been awakened; there have been times that I have been carried out of myself by something greater than myself and to that something I gave myself. Has this great something been God? Maybe after all, I have been religious for a number of years, and am now only becoming aware of it.[39]

King recorded the impact of Brightman and DeWolf, personally and intellectually, on his thought in these words:

> Both men greatly stimulated my thinking. It was mainly under these teachers that I studied personalistic philosophy – the theory that the clue to the meaning of ultimate reality is found in personality. This personal idealism remains today my basic philosophical position. Personalism's insistence that only personality – finite and infinite – is ultimately real, strengthened me in two convictions; it gave me metaphysical and philosophical grounding for the idea of a personal God, and it gave me a metaphysical basis for the dignity and worth of all human personality.[40]

For King, personalism validated the notion that experience rather than intellectual reflection should be the basis of religious belief. "It is through experience that we come to realize that some things are out of harmony with God's will," he wrote in reference to personalism. "No theology is needed to tell us that love is the law of life and to disobey it means to suffer the consequences."[41] King's adoption of personalism as a theological orientation enabled him to reject abstract conceptions of God while continuing his search for cogency and intellectual sophistication.

Robert L. Franklin offers the notion of the *Integrative Person* as that which best captures the essence of King's ongoing development and thinking. [42] In the summer of 1958, King was invited to deliver two devotional addresses at the first National Conference on Christian Education of the United Church of Christ, at Purdue University. In one of the addresses, "The Dimensions of a Complete Life," he offered a vision of human fulfillment by using geometry as an organizing paradigm. He conceived the complete life to be a process, a quest, rather than an achievement. This is clearly evident in Franklin's construct of the *Integrative Person*. Inspired by the geometric perfection of the New City of God described in the Book of Revelation (chapter 21), King suggested that the complete life was analogous to a cube. Each of its three dimensions represents a significant individual/personal commitment. (1) The length of life corresponds to a person's inner concern for her/his own welfare and development; (2) the breadth of life pertains to concern for the welfare of others; and (3) the height of life refers to concern for reconciliation and communion with God.

With regard to the length of life, King stressed that it "… is not its duration or its longevity, but it is the push forward to achieve life's personal ends and ambitions." It is the inward concern for a person's own welfare and the realization of his own purposes. The individual is concerned with developing (their) inner powers. It is that dimension of life in which the individual pursues personal ends and ambitions. He said, "Love yourself, if that means rational and healthy self-interest. You are commanded to do that."[43]

King pointed out that length without breadth, the second dimension of the complete life, is like a self-contained tributary having no outward flow to the ocean. Stagnant, still and stale, it lacks both life and freshness.[44] The "I" cannot attain fulfillment without the "thou." For its full development, the self needs other selves. Paul Tillich observed that only a "thou" can make man realize he has an ego.[45] The breadth of life is that dimension of life in which we are concerned about others. An individual has not started living until one can rise above the narrow confines of individualistic concerns to the broader concerns of all humanity.

Finally, there is a third dimension to a complete life - the height of life. King pointed out that some people never get beyond the first two dimensions, and thus life remains incomplete. They develop their inner powers, and they love humanity, but they stop right there. Without God, even the most brilliant achievements on the other two dimensions soon prove to be empty and disillusioning. King pointed out that if persons are to live the complete life they must reach up and discover God.[46]

In challenging everyone to live an integrative /complete life of *agape* (God's unconditional love), King developed the Christian implications of the second and third dimensions of the complete life, and in effect maintained that at times the practice of *agape* may require suspension of the first dimension, immediate self-interest. For King, it is in persons' attainment of the three dimensions of life that the *imago Dei* (image of God) can be most fully seen.

### D. Walter Rauschenbusch

At Crozer Theological Seminary, King continued a search begun at Morehouse for a theological-philosophical method to eliminate social evil. According to Sylvie Laurent in *King and the Other America*, a progressive theology, combined with social justice politics, nourished and shaped King's calling, which he defined eloquently when as a nineteen-year-old first-year student at Crozer Seminary, he predicated: "My mission is to deal with unemployment, slums and economic insecurity."[47] Among others, he studied the history of philosophy and the thought of Walter Rauschenbusch. In his first book, *Stride toward Freedom*, King acknowledged that Rauschenbusch's *Christianity and the Social Crisis* left "an indelible imprint" on his thinking by providing him with a theological base for the social concern he had developed as a result of his early experiences.[48]

One of the manifestations of evangelical liberalism was the Social Gospel movement. King's consistent synthesis and appropriation of the liberal social gospel perspective of Rauschenbusch can be viewed within the context of the complex nature of the southern Black (often fundamentalist, yet liberation/transformation-oriented) Christianity of King's upbringing in the Baptist Church and community.

In his seminal work, *A Theology of the Social Gospel*, Rauschenbusch stated that "we have a social gospel." [49] For Rauschenbusch, the gospel of Christ, by its very nature is "social" and has communal implications. Rauschenbusch's ministry and work in New York City laid the foundation for a movement in many Protestant circles in the early and mid-20th century towards the predominant appropriation of socially concerned evangelical liberalism. Like Rauschenbusch, King would be led to assert that the gospel of Christ is, by its very nature, "social".

According to Gary Dorrien, the appropriation of the social gospel predated King by several decades among leaders in the Black churches. Long before he burst on the national scene in December 1955 there was an African-American tradition of social gospel Christianity that preached social justice politics in the way that King later personified.[50] Historically, the black social gospel was rooted in abolitionist black religion and the teaching of the Bible that God favors the poor and oppressed. It emerged from the ravages of the transatlantic slave trade, the birth of African-American Christianity and the legacy of the abolitionist tradition, addressing the crisis of a new era.[51]

In much of the social teaching of the black churches as institutions, there has been, and continues to be imbedded the ideological insistence on common ground as a theological, sociological and ethical frame of reference. In his book, *The Social Teaching of the Black Churches,* Peter Paris posits that two primary instruments of social reform and communal power employed by black churches have been: (1) the biblical idea of the parenthood of God and the kinship of all people, and (2) the constitutional idea that all people are created equally and endowed by their Creator with certain inalienable rights. Paris further asserts that neither violence nor colonization ever gained domicile in the black churches, even though a few people from time to time have pushed for such strategies. In their struggle against racism and classism, black churches have never understood themselves as a narrow self-interest group seeking their own satisfaction.[52]

King noted the impact of the thought of Rauschenbusch on his intellectual attraction and appropriation of the social gospel:

> ...Rauschenbusch gave to American Protestantism a sense of social responsibility it should never lose. The gospel at its best deals with the whole man, not only his soul but also his body, not only his spiritual well-being but also his material well-being. A

religion that professes a concern for the souls of men and is not equally concerned about the slums that damn them, the economic conditions that strangle them, and the social conditions that cripple them, is a spiritually moribund religion.[53]

King's views on the relationship between the church and society were significantly influenced by Rauschenbusch. Gary Dorrien posits that Rauschenbusch was the foremost intellectual influence on King.[54] Like Rauschenbusch, King firmly believed that the church should take the lead in programs of social action and societal change. The church should engage in combating injustices that people confront in the areas of housing, education, employment, transportation and healthcare. For King, it was essential for the church to recapture its prophetic vision, and to actively participate in the struggle for economic and racial justice, and peace in communities and among the nations of the world.

In arriving at a theological/philosophic construct for the social gospel, Rauschenbusch viewed religion as essentially ethical and social within the context of a prophetic framework. He outlined his perspectives on ethical and social religion in *Christianity and the Social Crisis*.[55] Rauschenbusch traced the historical roots of Christianity and argued that Jesus stood squarely in the tradition of the Old Testament prophets, and that Christianity was the direct heir of the priority assigned to the social dimension of life by the prophets of Israel. Moreover, whenever Christianity has attempted to change social and political conditions for the betterment of humankind, it has manifested its indebtedness to the social ideals of the Old Testament because they have made, when properly understood and interpreted, positive contributions to the development of democracy and social justice culture.[56]

The essence of the prophetic principle, according to Rauschenbusch, is the affirmation of historical relativity – everything in history stands under the judgment of God. For this reason the prophet cannot put a stamp of approval upon anything "as it is." The prophet must always point out the gap between the will of God and "the present things." No person who calls himself or herself a Christian can accept "things as they are"; instead, one must condemn them on the basis of the values enunciated by the prophets and Jesus.[57]

Rauschenbusch offered several corollaries of the prophetic model. One is the *inseparability of religion and ethics*. If one believes in the social gospel, any method of cultivating the spiritual life may be chosen provided it has an ethical outcome. Righteousness is what God commands; an ethical life is the appropriate act of worship; and the amelioration of social injustice is the goal of the religious person. Another corollary of the prophetic model of religion for Rauschenbusch is the *affirmation of the fundamental social character of religion*. He claimed that the social nature and dimensions of religions should be the major norm for evaluating religious systems.[58]

According to Rauschenbusch, "the Kingdom of God is not simply a matter of getting people to heaven, but of transforming the life on earth into the harmony of heaven."[59]

Rauschenbusch and other adherents of the Social Gospel movement promoted a progressive form of Christianity, which sought to address concrete spiritual and material needs of people.

In summary, the Social Gospel, as expressed by Rauschenbusch and others, involves several tenets, including:

1. God is on the side of the oppressed. The most vulnerable are to be given preference.

2. Salvation is a material concern as much as it is a spiritual concern. The gospel beckons believers to work for improved housing, education, healthcare, transportation, employment and other benefits for the less fortunate.

3. Salvation is a communal as much as an individual concern. To honor God, people must put aside their own earthly desires and help other people, especially the needy.

4. The Social Gospel is rooted in the social-ethical teachings of Christ (Luke 4:18-19; Matthew 5; Matthew 25). The way of Christ is to emulate the life of Jesus Christ.

5. There is an interest in the systematic redistribution of power (social, economic and political). There also is a concern for the redistribution of wealth. In the social gospel, the purpose of wealth is not to accumulate and hoard it, but to share it with other, less fortunate people.

6. The prophetic voice is equally as important as the priestly, and Christians (ministers and laity) should be engaged in the public square.

7. The church is not a servant or master of the state, but a critic and moral conscience of the state. This was clearly intimated later by Dietrich Bonhoeffer, Martin Luther King Jr., Fannie Lou Hamer, Oscar Romero, Desmond Tutu, and other adherents of a form of the social gospel. King similarly stated that "the church must be reminded that it is not the master or servant of the state, but rather the conscience of the state. It must be the guide and critic of the state, and never its tool."[60]

## E. Reinhold Niebuhr

It was through a study of Walter Rauschenbusch and the social gospel that Martin Luther King, Jr. recalled that he learned, again, that "the gospel deals with the whole man, not only his soul but his body." His professors, however, told him that social gospel progressivism was out of touch with many of society's hard realities and injected him with a dose of Reinhold Niebuhr's "Christian realism."[61] King's respect for the writings of Niebuhr derived from the pleasure he felt in finding a theological stance that synthesized faith and intellect. In Niebuhr's Christian realism, King probably heard echoes of his father's fundamentalism, which affirmed the limits of human perfectibility. Niebuhr provided an intellectual rationale for King's recognition of the limits of liberal theology.

King wrote that he had become "so enamored of the insights of liberalism that I almost fell into the trap of accepting uncritically everything it encompasses."[62] After reading Niebuhr, King recalled becoming aware of the "depth and strength of sin" and:

... the complexity of man's social involvement and the glaring reality of collective evil. I realized that liberalism had been all too sentimental concerning human nature and that it leaned toward a false idealism. I also came to see that the superficial optimism of liberalism concerning human nature overlooked the fact that reason is darkened by sin. The more I thought about human nature, the more I saw how our tragic inclination for sin encourages us to rationalize our actions. Liberalism failed to show that reason by itself is little more than an instrument to justify man's defensive ways of thinking. Reason, devoid of the purifying power of faith, can never free itself from distortions and rationalizations.[63]

Niebuhr's Christian realism or "realistic theology" was most fully explicated in his seminal work, *Moral Man and Immoral Society* (1932). Christian realism was a more moderate reaction to liberalism than the more severe reactions of the neo-orthodoxy of Karl Barth, Emil Brunner and others. Also, Christian realism retained a far greater concern for social ethics. King noted his affinity with the thinking of Niebuhr in seeking to distinguish neo-orthodoxy and liberalism, from Christian realism:

Niebuhr's great contribution to contemporary theology is that he has refuted the false optimism characteristic of a great segment of Protestant liberalism, without falling into the anti-rationalism of the continental theologian Karl Barth, or the semi-fundamentalism of other dialectical theologians.[64]

Niebuhr argued that the ethical considerations which govern relations between individuals are not the same as those which govern inter-group relations. One may be willing to make all kinds of personal sacrifices to live the ethical life (moral man), but the same sacrifice may be too much to expect of a body politic (immoral society). As an individual, one may have the ability to face emaciating and abusive conditions nonviolently as a symbol of protest against politics, but the same individual may decide that a more violent response is required if those conditions threaten his/her fellows. A group is not just the sum total of its individual members. A group can have a consciousness and value system which differs from those of individual members.[65]

For King, a religion that focuses exclusively upon the individual is a truncated form of religion. He applauded Niebuhr's rigorous analysis of "the fundamental weaknesses and inevitable sterility of the humanistic emphasis" of liberalism in the twentieth century.[66] He was drawn to Niebuhr's economic and moral analysis of capitalism, such as the notion that modern industrial civilization was responsible for "appalling injustices," particularly the "concentration of power and resources in the hands of a relatively small wealth class."[67] Injustices are inherent in human society, Niebuhr argued, because humans engaged in collective activity are essentially immoral, whereas individuals acting on their own possess a moral conscience. Niebuhr sought to resolve the tension between "moral man and immoral society" by reinterpreting the traditional Christian notion of *agape,* or divine love.[68] Agreeing with Niebuhr's analysis, King stated that *agape* may not be achievable in an immoral society but "remains a leaven in society, permeating the whole and giving texture and consistency to life."[69]

The proponents of Christian realism argued that the biblical understanding of human nature, symbolized by the myth of the Fall, is a far more accurate and realistic understanding of the human situation than either the pessimism of Christian orthodoxy or the optimism of Christian liberalism. The one objective and empirically verifiable base from which most realistic theologians operated because they thought it could be clearly documented as a fact of human experience was the doctrine of original sin (i.e., the egotistic predicament of every human being).

With regard to Niebuhr's critique of the optimistic doctrine of humankind in Protestant liberalism, King asserted:

> Niebuhr has extraordinary insight into human nature, especially the behavior of nations and social groups. His theology is a persistent reminder of the reality of sin on every level of man's existence…While I still

believed in man's potential for good, Niebuhr made me realize his potential for evil as well.[70]

In short, Christian realism was the theological expression of a general revolt against the romanticism, idealism and liberalism of the nineteenth century. Niebuhr was the moving spirit of theological realism. King was an heir of this new school of thought through the influence of Reinhold Niebuhr.[71] By the time King wrote *Where Do We Go from Here: Chaos or Community?* in 1967, he had arrived at a position on the relationship among power, justice and love which was similar to that of Niebuhr. Although there were differences in emphasis and mode of expression at some points, the substance was quite similar. King understood and agreed with the necessity of power, as Niebuhr had stated it, to facilitate constructive change.[72] He concluded that it was utopian to believe that ethical appeals and persuasion alone will bring about justice. This does not mean that ethical appeals must not be made. It simply means that those appeals must be undergirded by some form of constructive coercive power." [73]

Niebuhr believed life must not only be governed by a concept of love, but also by a distinct and profound concept of justice.[74] For Niebuhr that justice could be a fulfillment of love. He said, "Yet the law of love is involved in all approximations of justice, not only as the source of the norms of justice, but as an ultimate perspective by which their limitations are discovered."[75]

King remained particularly receptive to Niebuhr's criticism of love and justice as conceived in both liberal and orthodox theology. In orthodoxy, "individual perfection is too often made an end in itself," whereas liberalism "vainly seeks to overcome injustice [through] purely moral and rational suasions." Liberalism, King wrote, "confuses the ideal itself with the realistic means which must be employed to coerce society into an approximation of that ideal."

King agreed with Niebuhr's emphasis on making realistic moral choices and with Niebuhr's social analysis, but he believed that Niebuhr lacked an adequate explanation of how *agape* operates in human history: "He fails to see that the availability of the divine *agape* is an essential [affirmation] of the Christian religion."[76] Despite his general affinity with Niebuhr's thinking, King remained concerned with Niebuhr's apparent overemphasis on the corruption of human nature. King said, "His pessimism concerning human nature was not balanced by an optimism concerning divine nature. He (Niebuhr) was so involved in diagnosing man's sickness of sin that he overlooked the cure of grace."[77]

## CHAPTER THREE

## SOUL FORCE - MOHANDAS GANDHI, MARTIN LUTHER KING, JR. AND THE POWER OF LOVE

Mohandas K. Gandhi was one of the few persons in modern history to lead in the struggle for human progress simultaneously on moral, religious, political and cultural fronts. His life and praxis of nonviolence impacted many persons in India and around the world in the promotion of peace and love, with justice, and continues to impact persons, institutions and nations today. Gandhi's thought and praxis on nonviolence had an indelible impact on American religious leaders of the early to middle 20th century like Mordecai Johnson, Howard Thurman and Martin Luther King, Jr.

In assessing Gandhi's impact, Huston Smith, in *The World's Religions* offered that "the face of Hinduism for the West is Mohandas Gandhi." According to Smith, "Most responsible for awakening the West to the realities of the East (and the beauty of Hinduism) was a little man who weighed not much more than a hundred pounds and whose possessions when he died totaled two dollars.[78] Gandhi's face is one of the most universally recognized around the world. As it regards Gandhi's national and global impact, E. Stanley Jones wrote:

> I have said that Gandhi was India, but that has to be corrected: Gandhi *is* India. It is no mere chance that his ashes were scattered in the 114 rivers of India. For he belonged to all India – was bone of its bone, blood of its blood, and is now ashes of its ashes. In Gandhi, an ancient civilization, bound and clamped by cramping custom and mental and physical chains, came to renaissance, a new birth, and was free. When [men] saluted Gandhi, they saluted a new India.[79]

Gandhi's title, "Mahatma" – "whose essence of being is great" as the title "mahatma" would be literally translated, was befitting his life's achievements. Huston Smith asserted that the most notable achievement for which the world credited Gandhi was the peaceful British withdrawal from India. What is not as well-known is that among his own people, he lowered a barrier thought by many to be much more formidable than that of British colonialism in India, racism in the United States or Apartheid in South Africa - renaming and redefining the lowest caste of Dalits and "untouchables" in India as "*harijans*", God's children, and raising them to human status. And in doing so he provided the nonviolent strategy as well as the inspiration for Martin Luther King, Jr.'s comparable civil rights movement in the United States.[80]

# I. Towards a Spirituality and Philosophy of Nonviolence

## A. Gandhi's Early Development

Mohandas Gandhi was born in India in 1869 into the Vaisa caste (merchants, farmers, and craftspeople).[81] His father, however, was involved in law and politics. His mother was a devout Hindu, and engaged in self-discipline, purification and other religious observances. Gandhi's India was dominated by British colonialism. In Rajkot, he experienced early segregation. The British reserved for themselves the best part of town; Indians were restricted to the slums. At school, he was taught in English, under the assumption that everything Indian was inferior. He disliked this arrangement, and he felt that Indians needed the pride of language, custom and history. With his pride of self and people, Gandhi studied both Sanskrit and Persian.[82]

When he decided to go to England to study law, Gandhi came up against the stark realities of the caste system, and racial and religious disintegration. His family told him that if he crossed the ocean to a foreign land, he would become an outcast. He, however, did not yield to this threat and vowed to be a Hindu wherever he was. A family priest intervened on his behalf and assured everyone that if Gandhi kept his vow, he could remain a Hindu. His treatment while in England led him to declare war against the strictures and harshness of the Indian caste system, and this conviction remained with him for the rest of his life.

In England, Gandhi's philosophy of nonviolence began to take shape. He studied the ideas of Hindus, Buddhists and Christians. He was moved as well by the writings of American authors like Ralph Waldo Emerson and Henry David Thoreau. Thoreau's ideas on civil disobedience were especially impressive to Gandhi. His encounter with the New Testament, especially with Jesus and the Sermon on the Mount, also had a profound impact on Gandhi's thinking.

As someone whose entire adult life was consumed with fighting against such injustices as racial discrimination in South Africa, British rule in India, and ugly social practices within his own society, Gandhi sought to develop an approach to how moral persons could and should act in such struggles. He found both the methods of rational discussion and violence – the traditional methods which appealed to people in addressing injustice – unsatisfactory to various degrees, and thus sought to discover an alternative and more powerful method.

Gandhi was particularly disturbed by the ease with which violence had been rationalized and used throughout history. He realized that violence was born out of frustration, and many who used it resorted to it only because they saw no other way to fight entrenched injustices, and that much of the blame for its use had to be laid at the doorsteps of a morally blind and narrow-minded dominant group.

He opposed violence on both ontological and moral grounds. From an ontological perspective, violence denied the fact that all human beings had souls, and that they were capable of appreciating and pursuing good. Furthermore, in order to be justified in taking the extreme step of harming or killing someone, one had to assume that one was absolutely right, and the opponent totally wrong, and that violence would definitely achieve the desired result.

On moral grounds, every successful act of violence encouraged the belief that it was the only effective way to achieve the desired goal, and developed the habit of turning to violence every time one ran into opposition. Society thus turned to violence, and it never felt compelled to explore alternatives. Violence also tended to generate an inflationary spiral. Every successful use of violence blunted the community's moral sensibility and raised its threshold of violence, so that over time, an increasingly larger amount of violence became necessary to achieve the same results. In Gandhi's view the facts that almost every revolution in history has led to terror, devoured its children, and failed to create a better society were proof that the traditional theory of revolution was fatally flawed.

In his view violence also tended to be based on the narrow premise that the perpetrator was in some way morally superior, while the object of violence was in some way contradistinctively morally inferior.

Gandhi concluded that since the two methods (rational discussion and violence) of fighting against injustice were inadequate and deeply flawed, a third method was necessary. It should activate the soul, mobilize individuals' latent moral energies, appeal to both the head and heart, and create a climate conducive to peaceful resolution of conflict conducted in a spirit of mutual good will.

## B. Development of Satyagraha

Faith was at the center of Gandhi's life. He believed in God, and in truth. "What I want to achieve, what I have been striving and pining to achieve these thirty years," he wrote in his autobiography, "is self-realization, to see God face to face. I live and move and have my being in pursuit of this goal. All that I do by way of speaking and writing, and all my ventures in the political field, are directed to the same end." He saw the face of God in the poorest peasant and in the struggle of nonviolent resistance and love in the public realm. He sought to uncover truth at every turn and found that justice and nonviolence spring from the journey in truth. "You may be sent to the gallows, or put to torture, but if you have truth in you, you will experience an inner joy." Truth, for Gandhi, was the essence of life.[83]

The formative ideas of his philosophy began to take shape in the years he worked to better the social and economic conditions of Indians in South Africa. He spent 20 years of his life in South Africa as an acknowledged leader of the Indian people.[84] Rajmohan Gandhi, research professor at the Center of Policy Research, New Delhi, India suggested that much of Mohandas Gandhi's view on nonviolence can be traced to his personal experiences and early encounters with bigotry on his journey to South Africa in 1893.[85] Rajmohan Gandhi offered an account, depicted in the Attenborough film, of the well-known incident when

Mohandas Gandhi was ejected from the railway train at the station of Pietermaritzburg in 1893:

> The barrister trained in London, he was holding a first-class ticket and had just arrived in South Africa – he had been there hardly a week. Because he did not have the right skin color and did not move to the van compartment when asked, he was thrown out. Then he made a journey by train, coach, and train again, eventually arriving, via Johannesburg in Pretoria. Along the way he was roughly beaten on the coach because he refused to sit as ordered on the floor. He tried to spend the stopover night in Johannesburg in a hotel, but was told that there was no room. He had experiences that were not very pleasant. On a Sunday evening he arrived in Pretoria, his destination. Not sure of what lay ahead of him, and remembering that he could not get accommodations in Johannesburg, he wondered where he would spend his first night in Pretoria. He decided to consult the man who was checking tickets at the exit for ideas. While he was having this conversation, a Black American noticed the predicament of the young man from India (Gandhi was only 23 at this time), went up to Gandhi, and asked the young man if he could help.[86]

Gandhi explained his anxiety. The African American said, "I have an American friend, Mr. Johnston, who has a hotel in Pretoria. He might put you up." So Gandhi and this man, whose name was not known to him, walked from the station to the hotel. Gandhi described the incident in his autobiography, written 33 years later, but did not give the name of the Good Samaritan. At the hotel the man introduced Gandhi to Mr. Johnston, who said: "You can stay in the hotel if you are willing to eat in your room. If I took you to the dining room, the other guests might not like it." Gandhi hated conditions of this sort but he made the compromise. "All right," he said. A little later there was a knock on the door, and Gandhi thought it was a man with a tray. But it was Mr. Johnston himself, who said: "I have spoken to the other guests in the hotel and they are willing for you to eat in the dining room." As far as I know it was Gandhi's first encounter with Americans, one Black and the other White.[87]

Rajmohan Gandhi points out that it remains an interesting fact of history that the man who enabled Mohandas Gandhi to have a roof and a bed in Pretoria was an African American.[88] As is evident from a sketch of his early life, Gandhi was "born to rebel." His philosophy would inevitably be a philosophy for action. It was to be more than a philosophy for social engagement; it was to become a philosophy for social transformation. He came to believe that every person was of equal value, and that oppressed people should struggle for their equality. According to him, they must fight peacefully and they must not hurt others while doing so. He strongly believed that unjust laws should not be obeyed, but that people should not be violent in their attempts to change laws.

In 1907, Gandhi, who was still in South Africa, read Henry David Thoreau. In seeking to conceptualize Thoreau's philosophy, Gandhi borrowed the anglicized term "civil disobedience" which was more often referred to as "passive resistance." But he was not satisfied with either. Both, in his estimation, were too narrowly conceived; they appeared to be negative, passive and weak. They could easily denigrate into hatred and would likely opt, finally, for violence. Thus, civil disobedience and passive resistance became obsolete for Gandhi.

In a magazine called *Indian Opinion,* which he edited for a time in South Africa, Gandhi offered a small prize to be "awarded to the reader who invented the best designation for our struggle." One of his cousins, Maganlal Gandhi, produced a word that seemed almost right, *sadagraha,* which means "firmness in a good cause." Mohandas Gandhi corrected it to *Satyagraha... Satya* meaning "Truth"; *graha* meaning "firmness, tenacity, holding on." [89]

"I thus began," Gandhi says, "to call the Indian movement *Satyagraha,* that is to say the Force that is born in truth and love, or non-violence," and gave up the use of the phrase "passive resistance." On varying occasions, he called it "Soul Force", "Love Force" or "Truth Force." *Sat* in *Satyagraha* means "being," "that which is," "truth." For him, *Sat* was "the only correct and fully significant name for God. [90]

The conception of *Satyagraha* became fundamental to Gandhi's life and activity. [91] It is "truth-taking" or "the taking of vows of truthfulness." Its root/meaning is "holding on to truth" and, by extension, resistance to evil by nonviolent means. This "Truth Force" is possible because it excludes the use of violence, as humans are capable of grasping the truth (but not in an absolute sense) and are not competent to punish. Theologically, truth in an absolute sense is God or Ultimate Being.

In his writings, teachings and actions in South Africa, *Satyagraha* thus became manifest as a technique for action. It is not dogmatic; it is neither static nor substantial. It is, rather, a dynamic and spiritual concept, and a technique and process for action leading to personal and social transformation. In his view, *Satyagraha* is not intended to overwhelm one's opponent. It should not be used in an arbitrary way to rectify a situation. *Satyagraha* must be a last resort in an unbearable situation that merits the commitment of unlimited suffering. All would-be participants must be thoroughly prepared to know the factuality of the grievances being set forth. Participants must be willing to join in the conclusion that the cause is just and attainable, and they must be on the side of truth, which transcends facts. In other words, the truth being sought must be of such dimension that the practice of "soul-force" might give opponents concern. Opponents should be moved to seek the opportunity to change sides, and to approximate the higher goal or good that beckons all to become involved for human betterment and fulfillment.

A related concept used by Gandhi in the discussion of the meaning of nonviolent action was *ahimsa* (non-injury). This term is borrowed from the Jains. Jainism, founded by

Mahavira, is one of the oldest personally founded religions in India. The Jains were known for their doctrine of the non-injury of all forms of life. It was this religious concept of *ahimsa* that attracted Gandhi. Historically, Jains became merchants rather than farmers because they did not wish to destroy any form of (sentient) life. Even today, Jaina women wear veils over their noses and mouths to avoid breathing in any form of insect life.[92]

For Gandhi, *ahimsa* was the basic law of being. It can be used as the most effective principle for social action, since it is ingrained deeply in human nature and corresponds to humanity's innate desire for peace, justice, freedom and personal dignity. *Himsa* (violence or injury) is the opposite – it degrades, corrupts and destroys. It feeds on the tendency to meet force with force, hatred with hatred. This plan of action leads to progressive denigration. Nonviolence, on the other hand, heals and restores humanity's best nature, while providing the best means of restoring a social order of justice and freedom. *Ahimsa* is not preoccupied with the seizure of power as an end in itself; it is a way of transforming relationships in order to bring about a peaceful transfer of power.[93]

Gandhi was convinced of the power of nonviolence, through the principles of *Satyagraha* and *ahimsa,* as key to achieving the aims of peace. In 1926, he wrote:

> Nonviolence is the greatest force humanity has been endowed with. Truth is the only goal we have. For God is none other than Truth. But Truth cannot be, never will be reached except through nonviolence.

That which distinguishes us from other animals is our capacity to be nonviolent. And we fulfill our mission only to the extent that we are nonviolent and no more. We have no doubt many gifts. But if we do not serve the main purpose – the development of the spirit of nonviolence in us – they but drag us down lower than the brute, a status from which we have only just emerged. The cry for peace will be a cry in the wilderness, so long as the spirit of nonviolence does not dominate millions of men and women. An armed conflict between nations horrifies us. But the economic war is no better than an armed conflict. This is like a surgical operation. An economic war is prolonged torture. And its ravages are no less terrible than those depicted in the literature on war properly so called. We think nothing of the other because we are used to its deadly effects.[94]

Gandhi's conception of nonviolence, as expressed through *Satyagraha* and *ahimsa*, began with the spiritual disciplines of prayer, solitude and fasting. By avoiding power in all its forms of violence and control, and by renouncing the desire for immediate results, he discovered that one could be reduced to zero. From this ground zero of emptiness, the compassionate love of God - nonviolence – could grow. At this point, Gandhi wrote, the individual becomes "irresistible" and one's nonviolence becomes "all-pervasive." [95] Nonviolence, the power of the powerless, he believed, is the power of God, the power of truth and love that goes beyond the physical world into the realm of the spiritual. This power can overcome death, as God revealed through the nonviolence of Jesus, his crucifixion, and subsequent resurrection in the resisting community.[96]

Gandhi's experiments in Truth revealed that the mandate of the Sermon on the Mount – to love one's enemies – is of critical importance. In all of his public uses of nonviolence, he consistently expressed a desire for reconciliation and friendship with his opponent. He also always tried to stand in solidarity with the outcasts of society and to speak up for the rights of the marginalized. In India, such solidarity primarily meant taking the radical and scandalizing public stand on behalf of Dalits, the so-called untouchables. He conversely called them *harijans,* or "children of God," and begged his fellow Indians to banish untouchability from their hearts and lives.[97]

He warned against what he called the seven social sins, which served, in his estimation, ultimately to divide society into the powerful and the powerless. Gandhi identified these social sins as: (1) politics without principle, (2) wealth without work, (3) commerce without morality, (4) pleasure without conscience, (5) education without character, (6) science without humanity, and (7) worship without sacrifice. Jim Wallis, in *The Soul of Politics,* suggests that these social sins today… are the accepted practices of the life of the nation.[98]

William Shannon, in *Seeds of Peace: Reflections on Contemplation and Non-Violence,* asserted that no one has found an English equivalent for *Satyagraha.* Hence, we are still obliged to content ourselves with the word "nonviolence." But we need continually to make clear the positive meaning it intends to convey as a translation of *ahimsa.*[99]

For Gandhi, *Satyagraha,* and the related concept, *ahimsa,* became manifest as principled techniques for action towards nonviolence, peacemaking, community-building and a love-ethic that could lead to spiritual and social transformation. *Satyagraha* essentially aimed to penetrate the barriers of prejudice, ill-will, dogmatism, self-righteousness and selfishness, and to reach out to and activate the soul of the opponent. However degenerate, dogmatic or violent an individual might appear to be, according to the Satyagrahi, he had a soul, and hence the capacity to feel for other human beings and, on some level, acknowledge their common humanity. *Satyagraha* was in essence, "surgery of the soul," a way of activating "soul force" for Gandhi - and "suffering love" was the best way to accomplish this. As he put it:

> I have come to this fundamental conclusion that if you want something really important to be done, you must not merely satisfy the reason, you must move the heart also. The appeal of reason is more to the head, but the penetration of the heart comes from suffering. It opens up the inner understanding in man. Suffering is the badge of the human race, not the sword.

Gandhi explained the effectiveness of *Satyagraha* in terms of the spiritual impact of suffering love. The Satyagrahi's love of his opponent served as a disarming mechanism, defusing the opponent's feelings of anger and hatred, and mobilizing his higher nature. And the Satyagrahi's uncomplaining suffering denied his opponent the pleasure of victory.

In summary, Mohandas Gandhi's conceptions of *Satyagraha* and *ahimsa* can essentially be capsulized in the following nine observations:

*1.* Mohandas Gandhi was convinced that the power of nonviolence is the key to achieving the aims of peace. In 1926, he wrote, "Nonviolence is the greatest force with which humanity has been endowed. Truth is the only goal we have. For God is none other than Truth. But Truth cannot be, never will be reached except through nonviolence."

*2.* In 1907, Gandhi devised the Sanskrit term *Satyagraha,* with *sat* meaning "Truth", and *graha* meaning "firmness, tenacity, holding on." For him, this is Force that is born in truth and love, or non-violence." He thus gave up the use of the phrase "passive resistance." On various occasions, he called *Satyagraha,* "Soul Force", "Love Force" or "Truth Force."

*3.* The conception of *Satyagraha* became fundamental to Gandhi's life and activity. It is "truth-taking" or "the taking of vows of truthfulness." Its root/meaning is "holding on to truth" and, by extension, resistance to evil by nonviolent means.

4.  This "Truth Force" is possible because it excludes the use of violence, because humans are capable of grasping the truth (but not in an absolute sense) and are not competent to punish. Theologically, "Truth" in an absolute sense is God or Ultimate Being.

5.  A related concept used by Gandhi in the discussion of the meaning and practice of nonviolent action was the principle of *ahimsa* (non-injury). This term is borrowed from the Jains. Jainism, founded by Mahavira, is one of the oldest personally founded religions in India.

6.  For Gandhi, *ahimsa* was the basic law of being. It can be used as the most effective principle for social action since it is ingrained deeply in human nature and corresponds to humanity's innate desire for peace, justice, freedom and personal dignity. *Himsa* (violence or injury) is just the opposite – it degrades, corrupts and destroys.

7.  For Gandhi, *Satyagraha* was a primary technique for social action. It is not intended to overwhelm one's opponent. It should not be used in an arbitrary way to rectify a situation. *Satyagraha* must be a last resort in an unbearable situation that merits the commitment of unlimited suffering.

8.  *Satyagraha and ahimsa* were essential tools for Gandhi in the fight against what he deemed to be the

seven social sins, which served ultimately to divide society into the powerful and the powerless. He identified these seven social sins as: (1) politics without principle, (2) wealth without work, (3) commerce without morality, (4) pleasure without conscience, (5) education without character, (6) science without humanity, and (7) worship without sacrifice.

**9.** Gandhi's concept of *Satyagraha,* or Soul-Force (or Truth-Force), was understood almost immediately as "love-force" by Martin Luther King, Jr. and others. Like Howard Thurman and Mordecai Johnson, King saw a direct connection between Truth and Love, and like Gandhi, essentially equated the two. He saw in Gandhi the means by which the love-ethic in the teachings of Jesus – especially in the Sermon on the Mount - could become effective for social transformation. King stated, "As I read, I became fascinated by (Gandhi's) campaigns of nonviolent resistance…. The whole concept of *Satyagraha*... was profoundly significant to me… I came to feel that this was the only morally and practically sound method open to oppressed people in their struggle for freedom."

## C. *Satyagraha, Ahimsa and the Practice of Nonviolence*
Gandhi saw national self-respect as a religious and spiritual virtue. India was the embodiment of such truth and virtue to him. However, he knew well that national self-

respect could cloak cruelty and hatred. He was a strong Indian nationalist. A core of nationalism always resided in him, rallying Indians, inspiring colonized people everywhere to rise above the social ill and violence that was so much a part of Indian reality under British domination. He said in 1940: "my mission is to convert every Indian, whether he is a Hindu, Muslim or any other, even Englishmen and finally the world to nonviolence for regulating mutual relations whether political, economic, social or religious." The phrase "even ...and finally" revealed his priority towards serving and leading Indians to liberation. "I can't find Him apart from the rest of humanity," he said. "My countrymen," he added, "are my nearest neighbors." He had to serve people if he was to serve God; and his nearest neighbors were Indians. He said in 1931, "My nationalism, fierce though it is, is not exclusive, is not devised to harm any nation or individual."[100]

Gandhi realized that the spirituality of nonviolence begins within persons, and moves out from there. The life of active nonviolence is the fruit of an inner peace and spiritual unity already realized in us, and not the other way around... through our personal, inner conversion, our own inner peace, we are sensitized to care for God, ourselves, each other, for the poor, and for the world. He taught that nonviolence does not mean passivity. It is the most daring, creative and courageous way of living, and it is the only hope for the world. Nonviolence demands creativity. It pursues dialogue, seeks reconciliation, listens to the truth in opponents, rejects militarism, and allows God's Spirit to transform us socially and politically.[101]

Nonviolence is the essence of truth; one cannot seek truth, Gandhi asserted, and continue to participate in violence and injustice within one's heart and in the world. It is the only power that overcomes evil. "Nonviolence is the greatest and most active force in the world... One person who can express nonviolence in life exercises a force superior to all the forces of brutality... Nonviolence cannot be preached. It has to be practiced," he insisted. "If we remain nonviolent, hatred will die as everything does, from disuse."[102]

The first commitment of a nonviolent person is to the truth, according to Gandhi. Quoted by Thomas Merton, Gandhi summed up the heart of his teaching about nonviolence: "The way of peace is the way of truth." He even said: "Truthfulness is more important than peacefulness... A truthful person cannot long remain violent." He offered his reason for saying this: "A person will perceive in the course of his research that he has no need to be violent, and he will further discover that so long as there is the slightest trace of violence in him, he will fail to find the truth he is searching for." At the deepest level of our being we are in touch with God and therefore with truth itself. That is why at the core of our being we are nonviolent..." [103]

He viewed the problem of violence as being rooted in the hearts of men and women. Thus, the means of realizing nonviolence and peace were through transforming the hearts of persons. In 1926, he stated:

I observe, in the limited field in which I find myself, that unless I can reach the hearts of men and women, I am able to do nothing. I observe further that so long as the spirit of hate persists in some shape or other, it is impossible to establish peace or to gain our freedom by peaceful effort. We cannot love one another if we hate Englishmen. We cannot love the Japanese and hate the Englishmen. We must either let the Law of Love rule us through and through or not at all. Love among ourselves based on hatred of others breaks down under the slightest pressure. The fact is, such love is never real love. It is an armed peace. And so it will be in this great movement in the West against war. War will only be stopped when the conscience of humankind has become sufficiently elevated to recognize the undisputed supremacy of the Law of Love in all the walks of life. Some say this will never come to pass. I shall retain the faith till the end of my earthly existence that it shall come to pass.[104]

In 1929, Nobel Peace Prize recipient John Mott met Gandhi in India. Mott asked: "What causes you solicitude, concern, for the future of India?" That was on the eve of Gandhi's Salt March to the Sea, so that he was close to a high point in his freedom movement. Gandhi responded: "Our apathy and hardness of heart, if I may use the biblical phrase, toward the masses and their poverty."[105]

Mott also asked him about what India was meant to contribute to the world. Gandhi answered: "Nonviolence, which the country is exhibiting at the present day on a scale unprecedented in history." He added that nonviolence has "so permeated our people that an armed revolution has almost become an impossibility in India, not because, as some would have it, we as a race are physically weak, for it does not require much physical strength so much as a devilish will to press a trigger to shoot a person, but because the traditions of *ahimsa* (nonviolence/non-injury) have struck deep roots among the people."

Once two of Gandhi's close friends, Charles F. Andrews and Rabindranath Tagore, who had won a Nobel Prize for literature in 1913, expressed their unhappiness at one of Gandhi's methods in the nonviolent battle for freedom: the burning of foreign cloth. Tagore and Andrews said to Gandhi: "How can you do this? You are burning something valuable and beautiful." Gandhi gave his answer: "I want to care for the starving Indian peasant. He has nothing. I want him to spin and weave and to make cloth. Nobody will buy his cloth if mass-produced cloth from Manchester is sold in India." Also, said Gandhi: "Indians hate the British. I want to deflect their hate from people to things."

It is known that some Christians in England strongly urged Gandhi to convert to Christianity. He did read the Bible carefully. He found the Old Testament to be more difficult than the New Testament. Jesus, and the Sermon on the Mount impressed him more than any other part of the Christian Scriptures. John Dear intimates that "Gandhi disciplined himself to read daily from the Sermon on the

Mount, and live according to those teachings. Because of this commitment, he helped liberate both South Africa and India from systemic violence and showed the world the power of active nonviolence. In the process, Gandhi, a Hindu, became a Christ-like figure, "the greatest Christian of modern times," according to Martin Luther King, Jr."[106]

Gandhi never was convinced that it was necessary to abandon Hinduism for Christianity, however. He could not accept Christianity as a perfect religion. He also saw defects in Hinduism but, for him, Hinduism was all that was necessary to satisfy his soul. He had some leanings toward Christianity, but was never moved to make an all-out commitment to it.

Nevertheless, throughout his life, Gandhi was able to defend the best that he had gleaned from the study of Christianity. He urged people to live more like Jesus Christ, practice the Christian faith without adulterating it or toning it down, and to emphasize love and make it the driving force of life and action. It is not surprising that he asserted that his encounter with Christianity made him a better Hindu. His attention to some of the noblest principles of Christianity enriched his life as a religious person. Although he remained a Hindu, his understanding and expression of religious experience was more profound due to his engagement with Christianity.

## II. Gandhi's Engagement with African-American Religious Traditions

Many African-American leaders went to India beginning in the 1930s seeking Mohandas Gandhi's advice and to study his nonviolent method, with Howard and Sue Bailey Thurman, and Edward and Phenola Carroll being the first African Americans to meet personally with Gandhi in 1936.

In 1935, during his tenure at Howard University, Thurman, then the Dean at Andrew Rankin Memorial Chapel and Professor of Religion, and his wife Sue Bailey Thurman were asked to be members of a delegation on a "Pilgrimage of Friendship" to India, Ceylon and Burma. Thurman's participation was considered important because "in a country divided by religious beliefs into 'Touchables' and 'Untouchables', rich and poor, the testimony of representatives from another country's minority group might be far-reaching."[107]

Howard Thurman and the delegation lectured and discussed issues at 45 academic centers in these three countries from October 1935 through the spring of 1936. He was questioned continually about the compatibility of Christianity with black people's struggle for human dignity in America. White Christians and churches had a history of being insensitive to black people's worth and freedom. Thurman answered these queries by distinguishing American Christianity from the religion of Jesus. Despite this clarification, he admitted that:

All answers had to be defensive because there was not a single instance known to me in which a local church had a completely integrated membership. The color bar was honored in the practice of the Christian religion. From a 10,000-mile perspective, this monumental betrayal of the Christian ethic loomed large and forbidding.[108]

Embarking on "a serious intellectual quest for a method to eliminate social evil," while on their trip to India, the Thurmans and Carrolls had asked for a chance to visit with Gandhi. (Rev. Edward Carroll would eventually become one of the first African-American bishops in the United Methodist Church, elected in 1972). Gandhi had written welcoming them. Remarkably, he broke his fast for the duration of the delegation's visit. The delegation met for several hours with Gandhi in Bardoli, India. When the four Americans arrived, Gandhi went out of his way to greet them. He didn't always do that with visitors. His secretary, Mahadev Desai, told Howard Thurman that he had never seen Gandhi greet visitors so warmly in his many years with him.

By all accounts, Thurman's conversation with Gandhi represented the first formal exchange between an African-American religious leader and the great Indian prophet of nonviolent revolution. It was Gandhi's first opportunity to engage African Americans in discussion concerning their respective struggles for freedom. Often an outspoken critic of traditional Christianity, he believed that western interpretations of Christianity contributed to racial, economic and gender discrimination, and led to segregation of the world's people.

His encounter with Thurman became a profound aspect of Gandhi's spiritual life, offering him a view of Christianity which was, in many ways, transformational. During their discussion, which was largely centered on Gandhi's questions posed to Thurman concerning Christianity, parallels between the caste system of Hinduism and the exclusivity in the praxis of Christianity became apparent.

Thurman asked Gandhi to define nonviolence. Gandhi said he hoped it would be love in the Pauline sense, love as spelled out in Paul's second letter to the Corinthians, plus the struggle for justice. Thurman also asked Gandhi whether South African blacks had joined his nonviolence movement. Gandhi replied: "No, they hadn't." He said he deliberately did not want to amalgamate those two struggles at that time. He added that this was due to South Africans' lack of understanding of the meaning and methods of nonviolence. But Gandhi's work there had an impact on influential leaders in South Africa such as Albert Luthuli who, like Martin Luther King, Jr. was awarded the Nobel Peace Prize.

Thurman later recalled that Gandhi asked persistent, pragmatic questions about American Negroes, about the course of slavery, and how blacks had survived it.[109] Gandhi inquired about the plight of blacks in the United States with respect to issues such as economics, interracial marriage and politics.

In the course of his discussion with Gandhi, Thurman recalled the following: "One of the things that puzzled him (Gandhi) was why the slaves (in America) did not become Moslems. "Because", said Gandhi, "the Moslem religion is the only religion in the world in which no lines are drawn from within the religious fellowship. Once you are in, you are all the way in. This is not true in Christianity; it isn't true in Buddhism or Hinduism. If you had become Moslem, then even though you were a slave, in the faith you would be equal to your master."[110]

Gandhi asked his American visitors if they would sing a Negro spiritual for him. He was greatly moved as Sue Bailey Thurman sang two familiar Negro spirituals: "Were You There When They Crucified My Lord" and "We Are Climbing Jacob's Ladder." To all who heard them, these spirituals expressed the hopes and aspirations of the oppressed to climb higher and higher until freedom's goal has been reached.[111]

After hearing these spirituals, Gandhi said to the four: "Well if it comes true it may be through the Negroes (in America) that the unadulterated message of nonviolence will be delivered to the world."[112] In other words, by this time in 1936, he was not sure that it would be India that would deliver a workable model of nonviolence to the world, and he gave expression to a prophetic intuition that African Americans would lead in demonstrating and modeling nonviolence on a global scale. The American Civil Rights movement of the 1950s and 1960s would confirm Gandhi's inclination.

The conversation between Howard Thurman and Gandhi continued. Thurman inquired further about the nature of nonviolence. Gandhi replied:

... without direct, active expression of it, nonviolence to my mind is meaningless. One cannot be passively nonviolent. In fact, nonviolence is a term I had to coin in order to bring out the root meaning of *ahimsa*. In spite of the negative participle "non," it is no negative force. Superficially, we are surrounded in life by strife and bloodshed, life living upon life. But some great seer, who ages ago penetrated the center of truth, said, "It is not through strife and violence but through nonviolence that man fulfills his destiny and his duty to his fellow creatures." It is a force that is more positive than electricity, and more powerful than either. At the center of nonviolence is the force, which is self-acting. *Ahimsa* means "love" in the Pauline sense, and yet something more than love defined by St. Paul, although I know St. Paul's beautiful definition is good enough for all practical purposes. *Ahimsa* includes the whole creation, and not only humans. [113]

Thurman asked: "How are we to train individuals and communities in this difficult act?" Gandhi replied:

... through great study, tremendous perseverance, and thorough cleansing of one's self of all impurities. If for mastering the physical sciences you have to devote a whole lifetime, how many lifetimes may be needed for mastering the greatest spiritual force that mankind has ever known? But why worry even if it means several lifetimes? For, if this is the only permanent thing in life, if it is the only thing that counts, then whatever effort you bestow on mastering it is well spent. "Seek ye first the Kingdom of Heaven and everything else will be added unto you." The Kingdom of Heaven is *ahimsa.*[114]

Sue Bailey Thurman asked, "How am I to act, supposing my own brother was being lynched before my very eyes?" Gandhi responded:

There is such a thing as self-immolation. Supposing I was a Negro, and my sister was ravished by a white and lynched by a whole community, what would be my duty? I ask myself. And the answer comes to me: I must not wish ill to these, but neither must I cooperate with them. It may be that ordinarily I depend on the lynching community for my livelihood. I refuse to cooperate with them, refuse to touch food that comes from them, and I refuse to cooperate with even my brother Negroes who tolerate the wrong. This is the self-immolation that I mean. I have often in my life resorted to this plan. Of course, a mechanical act of starvation will mean nothing. One's faith must remain undimmed while one's life ebbs out minute by minute.[115]

In formulating his response to Gandhi's critique of Christianity, Howard Thurman began to integrate Gandhian principles of unity and nonviolent social change into his own

Christian pacifism and mysticism.[116] Thurman returned to the United States with "an enhanced interpretation of the meaning of nonviolence."[117] From Gandhi, "a man who (was) rooted in the basic mysticism of the [Hindu] Brahma," Thurman learned the life-affirming concepts of *ahimsa* and *Satyagraha*. He found in Gandhi a kindred mind and spirit who refused to think in terms of a disconnected Truth, God, or Ultimate reality but focused his attention on that which was pre-eminently practical and spiritual.[118]

In 1945, two other African Americans met Gandhi. One was Deton Brooks of the *Chicago Defender,* who asked Gandhi if he had a message for America. In his well-known response, Gandhi said, "My life is its message." Also in the summer of 1945, Frank E. Bolden of the National Negro Press Association went to interview Gandhi, who however, interviewed Bolden on the condition of Blacks in the United States. Wrote Bolden on his exchange with Gandhi: "All during our discussion I noticed the great Mahatma's face registering first sorrow, then disgust, then agreement, followed by humor, and ending in pleasure."[119]

### III. Gandhi's Influence on Martin Luther King, Jr.

Mohandas K. Gandhi provided a deep reservoir of ideas from which Martin Luther King, Jr. drank. King may not have been equipped with the most rigorous understanding of nonviolent principles if not for his exposure to Gandhi. Although he had been committed – at least to some degree - to the transforming ideals of nonviolence prior to encountering the thought of Gandhi, King's contact with

Gandhi would serve to codify his thinking with regard to nonviolence, while also serving as an impetus for King's ongoing search for the realization of what he deemed to be the "*Beloved Community*".

King's attraction to Gandhian thought was somewhat surprising when considered within the context of the intense study King had already undertaken of Western history and its religious, philosophical and ethical underpinnings. He had studied Bentham and Mill's utilitarianism, Marxism, Hobbes, Rousseau and Nietzsche, and had also taken seriously the thought of theologians like Walter Rauschenbusch, Reinhold Niebuhr and Paul Tillich. But it was in Gandhi's philosophy that King found a morally and practically sound method open to and efficacious for oppressed people in their struggle for freedom.

King's attraction to Gandhi's thought and theo-praxis can be traced to models of social activism inculcated throughout the southern Black church and culture, to which King had been exposed and enculturated during his earlier spiritual and intellectual development. His sense of justice, and a prophetic stance for peace and the *Beloved Community* were values transmitted to him within the common ethos of his upbringing, then reinforced through his intellectual development and engagement with Gandhi's method of nonviolence.

Undergirding King's interpretations and use of nonviolent resistance were the traditional black family and church. It was these that provided the context and foundation for King's effective use of nonviolent direct action.[120] He did his best work in the South where family and church traditions for blacks were strongest. The role of black educational institutions, especially historically black colleges and universities, should also be considered. From this spiritual and intellectual base, his influence became both national and international. Thus, he drew upon the long prophetic protest principles in the black church and community, and transformed them into an operational paradigm of liberation from race and class oppression. For King, this resource of black religious experience – and by extension black community - stood alongside the legacy of Jesus and Gandhi.

King had turned to a number of writers including Karl Marx, and found them to be not fully helpful. An address by Mordecai Johnson, then the President of Howard University, had alerted King to the significance of Gandhi's teachings and the potential value of *Satyagraha* and *ahimsa* while King was a student at Crozer Theological Seminary. Johnson was one of the greatest orators and preachers of his era, and always held his audiences spellbound. Johnson had just returned from India when King heard him lecture on Gandhi. King offered this account of Johnson's lecture, and his (King's) first encounter with Gandhi's thought, and its impact:[121]

> ...to my great interest, he (Johnson) spoke of the life and teachings of Mahatma Gandhi. His message was so profound and electrifying that I left the meeting and brought a half dozen books on Gandhi's life and works. Like most people, I had heard of Gandhi, but

C. *Anthony Hunt*

I had never studied him seriously. As I read, I became deeply fascinated by his campaigns of nonviolent resistance. I was particularly moved by the Salt March to the Sea and his numerous fasts. The whole concept of *Satyagraha* was profoundly significant to me. As I delved deeper into the philosophy of Gandhi, my skepticism concerning the power of love gradually diminished, and I came to see for the first time its potency in the area of social reform. Prior to reading Gandhi, I had about concluded that the ethics of Jesus were only effective in individual relationships. The "turn the other cheek" philosophy and the "love your enemies" philosophy were only valid, I felt, when individuals were in conflict with other individuals; when racial groups and nations were in conflict, a more realistic approach seemed necessary. But after reading Gandhi I saw how utterly mistaken I was.

King encountered Gandhi's thinking at a time when American civil rights leaders were in the midst of a profound intellectual and spiritual quest for a means of addressing social evils. He sought an ethical framework that could serve as the foundation for tackling massive social evils such as racism in America, and he became fascinated with and encouraged by Gandhi's campaigns of nonviolent social resistance against colonialism and the caste system in India. Mordecai Johnson's presentation on Gandhi convinced King that Gandhi's thought and action crowned his search, and would help him formulate his Christian understanding of nonviolence.

J. Deotis Roberts, in his paper "Moral Suasion as Non-violent Direct Action", asserts that William Stuart Nelson is also a key person in understanding the link between Gandhi and King.[122] Nelson was a graduate of Yale Divinity School, and studied in Paris and Berlin. He was an administrator at Shaw and Dillard universities before going to Howard University to work with Mordecai Johnson. At Howard, Nelson served as professor of theology and philosophy, dean of the divinity school and vice president of the university.

Nelson researched and reflected on nonviolence throughout his life. He studied in India on several occasions and was a personal friend of Mohandas Gandhi. For Nelson, nonviolence was an active protest against injustice. He can be seen as an important bridge between Gandhi and African Americans, and as a scholar, he devoted more attention to Gandhian nonviolence than any other African American. At Howard University, Nelson was also associated with Howard Thurman and Benjamin Mays, who was president of Morehouse College during King's student days.[123]

Nelson studied Hindu literature and traced in it the roots of nonviolence. He also studied the life of Mohandas Gandhi whom he met and marched with in India. He found the major influences shaping the Gandhian concept of nonviolence in a number of documents: *The Vedas, The Upanishads, The Ramayana, The Mahabharta, The Bhagavid-Gita, The Laws of Manu,* as well as in Jaina and Buddhist documents. His search led him to the writings of Leo Tolstoy, Henry David Thoreau, and many others. As a

Jaina and Buddhist theologian, Nelson also searched the Bible, especially the Sermon on the Mount, for clues to understanding Gandhi's philosophy.[124]

In 1947, Nelson visited Gandhi.[125] That was the year that India became independent, but in October and November 1946, Hindu-Muslim killings had started in India and what was to become Pakistan. Two or three days after Indian independence, in Calcutta, Nelson asked Gandhi: "Why is it that Indians who had more or less successfully gained independence through peaceful means are now unable to check the tide of civil war through the same means?" Gandhi replied that it was indeed a searching question, which he must answer. He confessed that it had become clear to him that what he had mistaken for *Satyagraha*, or holding on to truth, was not *Satyagraha,* but a weapon of the weak. Indians, he said, "harbored ill-will and anger" against their erstwhile rulers while claiming to resist them nonviolently. Their resistance was therefore "inspired by violence" and not by regard for the humanity in the British whom they should convert through *Satyagraha.* Gandhi asserted:

> The attitude of violence which we had secretly harbored, in spite of the restraint imposed by the Indian National Congress, now recoiled upon us and made us fly at each other's throats when the question of the distribution of power came up. It was the passivity of the weak and not the nonviolence of the stout in heart who would never surrender their sense of human unity and brotherhood even in the midst of

conflict of interests, and would never try to convert and not coerce their adversary.[126]

The mission and ministry of Martin Luther King, Jr. in Montgomery, Alabama beginning in 1954 gave him the opportunity to test the Gandhian principles of nonviolent social resistance and direct action (*Satyagraha and ahimsa*). It has been appropriately observed that "if Rosa Parks had not sat down, King would not have stood up." He was immediately drafted as the leader of the Montgomery Bus Boycott, which commenced on December 5, 1955. He pointed to the significance of Gandhi's teachings on the events in Montgomery during the 381-day campaign:

> When I went to Montgomery as a pastor, I had not the slightest idea that I would later become involved in a crisis in which nonviolent resistance would be applicable. I neither started the protest nor suggested it. I simply responded to the call of the people for a spokesman. When the protest began, my mind, consciously or unconsciously, was driven back to the Sermon on the Mount, with its sublime teachings on love, and the Gandhian method of nonviolent resistance. As the days unfolded, I came to see the power of nonviolence more and more. Living through the actual experience of the protest, nonviolence became more than a method to which I gave intellectual assent; it became a commitment to a way of life. Many of the things that I had not cleared up intellectually concerning nonviolence were now solved in the sphere of practical action.[127]

In the Montgomery Bus Boycott and protests of 1955-56, King saw the connection with Gandhi's nonviolence. "I had come to see early that the Christian doctrine of love operating through the Gandhian method of nonviolence was one of the most potent weapons available to the Negro in his struggle for freedom."[128] King said that a white woman who sympathized with the protest movement wrote a letter to the editor that was published in the *Montgomery Advertiser* comparing the bus protest with Gandhi's movement in India. Before long, people were talking about Gandhi in Montgomery. "People who had never heard of the little brown saint of India were now saying his name with an air of familiarity," King wrote.[129]

J. Deotis Roberts asserts that one important sign of the transformative power of Christianity upon Gandhi's Hindu faith is manifest in his interchangeable use of "Truth" and "Love."[130] In fact, according to Roberts, one might correctly refer to "truth-force" as "love-force." Gandhi viewed nonviolence as an expression of love that grows out of the central truth of one's inner being and the unity of all existence. Love is kindness, compassion and helpfulness. There is no room for hatred and violence in a world where truth is recognized, and love is practiced. Whereas violence calls forth violence, love calls forth love.

King saw the direct connection that Roberts suggests between Truth and Love, and like Gandhi, essentially equated the two. He saw in Gandhi the means by which the love-ethic in the teachings of Jesus - especially in the Sermon on the Mount - could become effective for spiritual and social transformation. For both Gandhi and King, ideas had practical consequences. The issue then is one of identifying what in their thought was behind their action, in light of what Roberts conceives as the "moral suasion" espoused by leaders like King.[131]

King also saw in Gandhi the insistence that it was not necessary to limit the Christian love-ethic to individual relationships; the love-ethic could be applied to conflicts between races, cultures, tribes and nations.

He discussed how his exposure to Gandhi helped him to reconcile in his thinking the power of pacifism and nonviolent social resistance as a force for change:

> My study of Gandhi convinced me that true pacifism is not nonresistance to evil, but nonviolent resistance to evil. Between the two positions there is a world of difference. Gandhi resisted evil with as much vigor and power as the violent resister, but he resisted with love instead of hate. True pacifism is not unrealistic submission to evil power (as Reinhold Niebuhr contends). It is rather a courageous confrontation of evil by the power of love, in the faith that it is better to be the recipient of violence than the inflictor of it, since the latter only multiplies the existence of violence and bitterness in the universe, while the former may develop a sense of shame in the opponent and thereby bring about a transformation and change of heart. [132]

In a very clear way, King stated his discovery, and the impact of Gandhi on his theo-praxis: "Gandhi gave me the *Method*, and Jesus gave me the *Message*." King pointed out his particular attraction to Gandhi's notion of the love-ethic:

> Gandhi was probably the first person in history to lift the love-ethic of Jesus above a mere interaction between individuals to a powerful and effective social force on a larger scale. Love, for Gandhi, was a potent instrument for social and collective transformation. It was in this Gandhian emphasis on love and nonviolence that I discovered the method for social reform that I had been seeking for so many months. The intellectual and moral satisfaction that I failed to gain from the utilitarianism of Bentham and Mill, the revolutionary methods of Marx and Lenin, the social contracts theory of Hobbes, the "back to nature" optimism of Rousseau, and the superman philosophy of Nietzsche, I found in the nonviolent resistance philosophy of Gandhi. I came to feel that this was the only morally and practically sound method open to oppressed people in their struggle for freedom.[133]

King felt that Gandhi was probably the first person in history to lift the love-ethic of Jesus Christ to a place where it could become an effective instrument for collective transformation. Thus, the method of social reform, which had eluded King and others in the quest for racial justice in America, was now found in the way that Gandhi understood and appropriated Truth (as Love) as expressed in *Satyagraha* and *ahimsa*.

In light of the widespread contemporary conflicts among races, ethnic groups and nations, it is important to revisit the universal insights of Gandhi, and their impact upon the thinking and praxis of the likes of Martin Luther King, Jr. King wrote and spoke out vehemently against hatred in the church and society, and under great duress, he opposed racism, poverty, and other matters of social, political and spiritual concern like the war in Vietnam. It cost him support among black and white national leaders. But, as a Christian theologian and ethicist, he felt compelled to apply the Gandhian philosophy of nonviolence to the conflict among nations, as he had done to the conflicts among races and classes in America. Just four days before his death, before an audience of more than 4,000, King spoke out against the Vietnam War at the Washington National Cathedral. Thus, one of King's final messages to our world in the nation's capital was against war, and for peace and nonviolence, as he urged persons and nations to diligently seek an alternative to war in the settlement of international disputes.

### Conclusion

In Mohandas Gandhi's writings, teachings and actions, *Satyagraha,* and the related concept, *ahimsa,* became manifest as techniques for action toward nonviolence, peacemaking, community-building and a love-ethic that could lead to spiritual and social transformation. With the ongoing proliferation today of violence, war, local and global conflict, terrorism and geopolitical discord, Gandhi's philosophy and praxis can be helpful in the discovery of nonviolent approaches to peacemaking, community-building, conflict resolution and social transformation in the 21$^{st}$ century, and beyond.

Amidst various forms of social disintegration that continue to afflict society today, *Satyagraha* and *ahimsa* can serve as means of helping humanity move towards higher goals of the common good, nonviolence, and peace with justice that beckon all persons to become involved in the quest for human betterment, fulfillment and the *Beloved Community*.

## CHAPTER FOUR

## *I'VE BEEN TO THE MOUNTAINTOP – THE PROPHETIC LIFE AND LEGACY OF MARTIN LUTHER KING, JR.*

The preaching, public ministry and practice of public theology of Martin Luther King, Jr. offer critical lenses through which can be seen the prophetic role of the preacher and leader in the 21st century. In as much as he was a Baptist preacher and pastor, along with being best known in the public sphere as a key leader of the American Civil Rights movement, King was a public theologian, bringing to bear his theological training on the social and political conditions of his time. For him, faith – what we believe about God, the universe and God's people – was to be acted out in ways that brought about not only spiritual growth, but social transformation.

For King, if the church was to be the church, it would engage in prophetic witness that would bring its spiritual, intellectual, social, economic and political resources to bear in ways that would affirm God's love, and be truly reconciling, redeeming, reforming and liberating.

In his preaching and praxis of ministry, King's particular prophetic concerns centered on addressing what he deemed to be the "triplets of evil" – racism, materialism/classism (economic inequality and poverty), and militarism (war). He articulated his overarching prophetic concern when he stated:

> "We must rapidly begin to shift from a "thing-oriented" society to a "person-oriented" society. When machines and computers, profit motives and property rights are considered more important than people, the giant triplets of racism, materialism, and militarism are incapable of being conquered.[134]

His prophetic witness is to be seen within the historical context of America, which has been fraught with racism since the arrival of the first Africans in America in 1619, the subsequent establishment of the nation in the late 18th century, and the ongoing struggle for equality for American blacks. Taylor Branch in *The King Years* asserts that:

> U.S. history has been marked and largely defined by political struggle over a "self-evident" truth asserted in the (1776) Declaration of Independence: that "all men are created equal." From the American revolution forward, that founding principle has ignited controversy over the role of free government to secure "civil rights". The phrase, which pertains literally to anyone's rights of citizenship, acquired a strong racial connotation through chronic upheavals over slavery and segregation, lasting more than a century before the Civil War of 1861-65. Even today, the civil rights cause is associated in common parlance with Americans of African descent.[135]

King's prophetic witness helped to spawn a religious and social movement unparalleled in American history. The demand for racial and social justice in the American South was the impetus for concomitant social and political movements across a number of sectors of society:

- The roots of the struggle for women's rights (feminism and womanism), the rights of gays, lesbians and transgendered persons (LGBTQI+), the rights of workers and the disabled, and the rights of those who are immigrants of various hues of brown, red, white and black can be traced to the prophetic witness of King.

- It was King who espoused a form of nonviolent social resistance and direct action that ultimately led to the passage of the Civil Rights Act (1964), the Voting Rights Act (1965), and the Immigration and Nationality Act (1965) by the United States Congress - all signed into law by President Lyndon B. Johnson.

- The epistemic foundations of affirmative action – however we might view it today – are rooted in King's prophetic vision of economic and social equality and justice throughout society.

- The King-led American Civil Rights movement served as an impetus and model for liberation and human rights movements across the globe – in Africa, Asia, Europe, and Central and South America.

In consistently arguing for God's preferential option and concern for the oppressed and poor, King's was essentially a liberation theology. James Cone writes of the impact of King's prophetic witness:

> As a prophet, with a charisma never before witnessed in this century, King preached black liberation in the light of Jesus Christ and thus aroused the spirit of freedom in the black community. To be sure, one may argue that his method of nonviolence did not meet the needs of the black community in an age of black power; but it is beyond question that it was King's influence and leadership in the black community which brought us to the period in which we now live, and for that we are in debt. His life and message demonstrate that the "soul" of the black community is inseparable from liberation, but always liberation grounded in Jesus Christ...[136]

Addressed in this chapter will be Martin Luther King, Jr.'s prophetic life and legacy, with particular focus on ways that churches, preachers, leaders and activists today might appropriate prophetic preaching and praxis within the context of 21st century realities in the churches and society. This analysis will entail three parts: (1) First, a brief overview of prophetic preaching and witness – what it is – will be offered. (2) Second, will be a review and analysis of King's prophetic preaching and witness. (3) Third, a model for prophetic preaching and witness, as gleaned from the preaching and ministerial practice of King will be offered, with particular focus on principles and implications for the 21$^{st}$ century churches and society.

## I.   *Afflicting the Comfortable: Prophetic Preaching, Leadership and Public Theology*

What are we speaking of when speaking of prophetic preaching and leadership?   When addressing the matter of the prophetic role of the preacher/leader, several questions must be asked.   How does the preacher/leader speak to the church and society with a prophetic voice?   From whence does the power and authority of the preacher/leader come? From whence has the power and authority of the preacher/leader derived over history?

What are the words that will "afflict the comfortable", speak truth to power, and speak truth in love? What words will speak to systemic evils in the churches and the world, and lead persons of faith in Christ, and even those who may not be Christians, towards spiritual and social transformation, and just action?

Are there words from the Lord today that will adequately and relevantly speak to increasingly complex social concerns, and lead to the wholeness of individuals and communities?

What words from the Lord speak to disparities in education, employment, healthcare, housing, safety, transportation and technology?   Are there words from the Lord that speak to drug trafficking and addiction, violence, gambling and abortion?   Are there words that speak to gender injustice, marriage inequality, human trafficking, misogyny towards girls and women, domestic violence, police brutality, anti-immigration, homelessness, war, domestic and foreign terrorism, global warming, environmental injustice, white supremacy, over-incarceration, xenophobia, homophobia, wage and wealth gaps, conspicuous consumption, materialism and greed?

What resources can the preacher/leader today draw upon to empower her or him to speak to and act against the abject poverty, racism, sexism, heterosexism and classism incumbent across much of society and extant in many communities?

Are there words from the Lord about Ferguson, MO, Cleveland, OH, Chicago, IL, Flint, MI, Baltimore, MD, and Dallas, TX? How might the preacher/leader speak to and act against the death inflicted upon the likes of Trayvon Martin, Michael Brown, Sandra Bland, Tamir Rice, Eric Garner, Koryn Gaines, Freddie Gray, Atatiana Jefferson and Botham Jean? Are there words from the Lord for Charleston, SC and Charlottesville, VA?

What happens when the preacher/leader is accused of mixing politics with religion? How can she/he preach and lead in the legacy and tradition of the likes of Jarena Lee, Harriet Tubman and Frederick Douglass... Fannie Lou Hamer and Adam Clayton Powell... Katie Canon and Jeremiah Wright?

Should it ever be the preacher's role to speak to issues of social and political concern, or are preachers only to speak of spiritual, priestly and pastoral matters? How might preachers today balance their pastoral and priestly functions, with prophetic voice?

### Defining Prophetic Preaching and Leadership

Prophetic preaching and leadership essentially pertain to that which calls persons, the church and socio-political structures back into relationship with God, and paves the way for the in-breaking of the kin-dom of God. Prophetic preaching and leadership are rooted in the Old Testament biblical traditions, and in the public ministries of the likes of John the Baptist. In the first chapter of Mark, we find the story of John the Baptist. *"And so John the Baptist appeared in the wilderness, preaching a baptism of repentance for the forgiveness of sins"* (Mark 1:4).

John's ministry was not based in the synagogue, but in the wilderness. He did not dress in the fine garbs of the priesthood, but in camel's hair. He was not trying to maintain religious order and the status quo, but was preaching a radical, prophetic word - a word of preparation for the coming of the Lord, and repentance for persons to turn their lives back to God. John's was a prophetic word that God was ready to shake things up, and make straight the crooked places and things in the peoples' midst.

It was generally the task of biblical prophets to speak to real spiritual and social conditions which existed among Hebrew people and their communities – and to call people back into covenant relationship with God. Thus, the biblical prophets stood with one foot in the past – reminding Israel of its history with God – and with the other foot in the future, reminding people of their current spiritual and social condition, and of God's promise and hope for their future. Biblical prophets also had one foot in the religious community, and the other foot in the public square. Thus, the paradigm for the biblical prophetic preacher is a dialectical paradigm which held in tension history, here and hope – past, present and promise.

Prophetic preaching and leadership also model the ministry of Jesus who engaged the religious and social concerns of his day. Jesus heralded his divine purpose and mission when he declared in Luke 4:18-19 that *'The 'Spirit of the Lord is upon me, for [God] has anointed me to bring good news to the poor. [God] has sent me to proclaim freedom for the prisoners and recovery of sight for the blind, to set the oppressed free, to proclaim the year of the Lord's favor."*

In his book, *The Politics of Jesus: Rediscovering the True Revolutionary Nature of Jesus' Teachings and How They Have Been Corrupted,* Obery Hendricks asserts that by the nature of who Jesus was, and how he ministered, he was a prophetic and political figure. Hendricks writes, "To say that Jesus was a political revolutionary is to say that the message he proclaimed not only called for change in individual hearts but also demanded sweeping and comprehensive change in the political, social and economic structures in his setting in life."[137] Hendricks proposes that seven political strategies characterize the prophetic and revolutionary politics of Jesus. These strategies are: (1)

Treat people's needs as holy. (2) Give a voice to the voiceless. (3) Expose the working of oppression. (4) Call the demon by name. (5) Save your anger for the mistreatment of others. (6) Take blows without returning them. (7) Don't just explain the alternative, show it.[138]

In *Jesus and the Disinherited,* Howard Thurman asks a haunting question (especially) for persons of faith. "What does Jesus of Nazareth have to say to those who have their backs against the wall?"[139] What did Jesus have to say about the way those who were poor and otherwise marginalized and disinherited in his day were treated? Jesus offered an answer:

> *"... for I was hungry and you gave me food, I was thirsty and you gave me something to drink, I was a stranger and you welcomed me, I was naked and you gave me clothing, I was sick and you took care of me, I was in prison and you visited me... and 'Truly I tell you, just as you did it to one of the least of these, you did it to me."* (Matthew 25:42-43)

Jesus' prophetic ministry essentially sought to transform lives and social structures. In *The Empowerment Church,* Carlyle Fielding Stewart asserts that Jesus' ministry demonstrated empowerment.[140] Stewart points to four specific ways that the ministry of Jesus proved to be a ministry of empowerment and, by extension, transformation. First, Jesus taught people foundational principles of spirituality that enabled them to see their own spiritual traditions in new ways and to conceptualize new possibilities of God in new spiritual frameworks. Secondly, Jesus' ministry transformed people's spiritual perception and understanding of God through personal revelation, intervention and interaction with people. Encountering Jesus meant that persons were compelled to alter their ideas of God. Thirdly, Jesus transformed the concept of people in relationship with God. They no longer viewed themselves as passive objects of God's will or as people wholly incapable of positively influencing their social environment and milieu. They saw themselves as co-intentional catalysts for positive change. Fourthly, Jesus directly, as well as vicariously, transformed communities by providing individuals with the spiritual elements of positive change and renewal. Not only did the recipients of Jesus' power and grace experience change within, but their communities were also changed by the power of their testimonies of Christ's work in their lives.

Prophetic preaching and leadership also involve moral imagination. Frank Thomas in *How to Preach a Dangerous Sermon* posits that Martin Luther King, Jr.'s prophetic preaching and leadership is an example of this, and can be best characterized and capsulized through a comprehension of the qualities of moral imagination to: (1) Envision equality and represent that by one's physical presence; (2) Show empathy as a catalyst or bridge to create opportunities to overcome the past and make new decisions for peace and justice; (3) Draw upon sources of wisdom and truth in ancient texts, the wisdom of the ages; and (4) Use the language of poetry and art that lifts and elevates the human spirit by touching the emotive chords of wonder, hope and mystery.[141]

Thomas ties moral imagination to Walter Brueggemann's conception of prophetic imagination. Thomas asserts that Brueggemann correctly and pointedly asserts that the prophet brings to light "public expressions of those very hopes and yearnings that have been denied so long and suppressed so deeply.[142] With regard to prophetic imagination, Walter Brueggemann, in *The Prophetic Imagination* offers this perspective:

> I understand imagination is no doubt a complex epistemological process, to be the capacity to entertain images of meaning and reality that are beyond the givens of observable experience. That is, imagination is the hosting of the "otherwise"... beyond the evident. Without that we have nothing to say. We must take risks and act daringly to push beyond what is known to that which is hoped for and trusted, but not yet in hand.[143]

Brueggemann posits that four characteristics emerge as indicators of prophetic ministry: (1) an "alternative community" is established, which is conscious of its unique identity and mission to others; (2) the prophetic insights are communicated in every activity of ministry, and they define sources of life and death for every context; (3) persons are helped in seeing the world as it really is, and to become fully sensitive to the hurt and pain experienced in life; and (4) prophetic ministry seeks to penetrate despair so that new futures can be believed in and embraced by us.[144]

Prophetic preaching and leadership speak holistically to the existential concerns of people and communities. They speak to the hurts and hopes, and ultimately challenge the status quo with the expectation of deliverance and liberation from oppression for God's people.

Marvin McMickle, in *Where have All the Prophets Gone?*, asserts that prophetic preaching and leadership shift the focus of a congregation from what is happening as a local church to what is happening to them as a part of society. McMickle asserts that there is a need to recover this prophetic tradition in light of four prevailing trends in much of preaching (and leadership) today -

- An unclear/narrow understanding of morality

- An overzealous preoccupation with praise and worship

- A false and narrow view of patriotism

- An unbalanced focus on prosperity and personal enrichment themes.

McMickle further asserts that prophetic preaching (and leadership) happens when the preacher/leader has the courage to speak truth to power not only inside the church building, but also in the streets, boardrooms and jail cells of the secular world, thus, the need for prophetic preaching and leadership today.

## II.  The Prophetic Legacy of Martin Luther King, Jr.

Martin Luther King, Jr. exhibited a form of local, national and international spiritual and socio-political concern that constantly called people of America and the world to rise above the ills of racial discord and class division, and move toward the realization of the *Beloved Community*.  Joseph Evans asserts that King used the "beloved community" as metaphor to describe his revelatory vision of democratic equality.  Of course, King adapts the notion from Josiah Royce, who once spoke in similar tones about the beloved community.  However, King ultimately reimagines Western culture and civilization as the beloved community.[145]

Tommie Shelby, in *To Shape the New World: Essays on the Political Philosophy of Martin Luther King, Jr.*, posits that King believed that racial injustice and economic injustice have always been linked in America.[146]  In addressing the race/class nexus in King's political philosophy, Shelby further asserts that in King's analysis of ghetto poverty in cities like Los Angeles and Chicago, like Jim Cow segregation, ghetto conditions are a threat to dignity.[147]

Although King's message is often depicted as being directed exclusively towards the betterment of conditions for African Americans – and the call for their freedom from racial injustice – a careful analysis of his message points to a concern for the "World House" and a vision of unity, peace and quality of life for all people – Jews, Protestants, Catholics, Muslims, and for the many nationalities, ethnic and religious groups present in America and around the world. There is clear evidence that King's broader prophetic concerns included all persons who were in some way marginalized, disenfranchised and oppressed.

For instance, while towards the end of his life, King's concern was certainly for the eradication of poverty for urban African Americans in cities like Chicago, Los Angeles and Memphis, TN, he expressed concern and worked for the betterment of all persons affected by poverty. A case in point is that his leadership in 1968 of the campaign on behalf of sanitation workers in Memphis would serve to impact the quality of life and economic well-being of all sanitation workers in that city, and serve as a launch point for what was to be a national poor people's campaign, with hopes of improving conditions for all poor people in America.

Like Jesus Christ in the temple that had become a den of thieves, King realized that the church and society are fertile ground for corruption. He viewed God as the source for overcoming such corruption. He shared this perspective on the connection of God with society:

> There is much frustration in the world because we have relied on gods rather than God. We have genuflected before the god of science only to find that it has given us the atomic bomb...We have worshipped the god of pleasure only to discover that thrills play out and sensations are short-lived. We have bowed before the god of money only to learn that there are such things as love and friendship that

money cannot buy and that, in a world of possible depressions, stock market crashes and bad business investments, money is a rather uncertain deity. These transitory gods are not able to save or to bring happiness to the human heart. Only God is able. It is a faith we must rediscover."[148]

King pointed out that the United States professes a balance between the whole and the individual, yet practices the exact opposite. He asserted that American society has a "schizophrenic personality." There are those who seek to convince us that only man is able. Their attempt to substitute a man-centered universe for a God-centered universe is not new.[149]

He viewed peace as the highest calling of the nation. In his last Christmas Eve sermon on December 24, 1967, he said:

> It is one of the strangest things that all the great military geniuses of the world have talked about peace. The conquerors of old who came killing in pursuit of peace – Alexander, Julius Caesar, Charlemagne, and Napoleon – were akin in seeking a peaceful world order. If you will read *Mein Kampf* closely enough, you will discover that Hitler contended that everything he did in Germany was for peace. And the leaders of the world today talk eloquently about peace. Every time we drop bombs in North Vietnam, President Johnson talks eloquently about peace. What is the problem? They are talking about peace as a distant goal, as an end we seek, but

one day we must come to see that peace is not merely a distant goal we seek, but that it is a means by which we arrive at that goal. We must pursue peaceful ends through peaceful means. One of the most persistent ambiguities we face is that everybody talks about peace as a goal, but among the wielders of power, peace is practically nobody's business. Many men cry "Peace! Peace!" but they refuse to do the things that make for peace. [150]

Much of King's hope for the nation would be capsulated in what he deemed to be the "American Dream". This became a prevailing theme for him. When he gave the commencement address at Lincoln University in Pennsylvania on June 6, 1961, he said that in order for the American public to realize "The American Dream", the first thing that needed to be affirmed is that the dream is universal, and comes out of the struggles of all persons.

His prophetic passion was perhaps most demonstratively and clearly articulated in his famous "I Have a Dream" speech, delivered on the steps of the Lincoln Memorial in Washington, DC on August 28, 1963. [151] At this – the largest protest march in the history of the United States to that date - King began his 17-minute address by drawing on the collective history and conscience of all of America:

Five score years ago, a great American, in whose symbolic shadow we stand today, signed the Emancipation Proclamation. This momentous decree came as a great beacon light of hope to millions of

Negro slaves who have shared in the flames of withering injustice. It came as a joyous daybreak to end the long night of their captivity.[152]

He continued by pointing America's sights to the condition of African Americans at the time of the 1963 March on Washington:

> But one hundred years later, the Negro still is not free; one hundred years later, the life of the Negro is still sadly crippled by the manacles of segregation and the chains of discrimination; one hundred years later, the Negro lives on a lonely island of poverty; one hundred years later, the Negro is still languishing in the corners of American society and finds himself in exile in his own land.[153]

King's plea to the nation continued:

> So we've come here today to dramatize a shameful condition. In a sense, we've come to our nation's capital to cash a check. When the architects of our republic wrote the magnificent words of the Constitution and the Declaration of Independence, they were signing a promissory note to which every American was to fall heir. This note was the promise that all men, yes black men as well as white men, would be guaranteed the unalienable rights of life, liberty and the pursuit of happiness.

> It's obvious today that America has defaulted on this promissory note in so far as her citizens of color are

concerned. Instead of honoring the sacred obligation, America has given the Negro a bad check; a check, which has come back marked "insufficient funds." We refuse to believe that there are insufficient funds in the great vaults of opportunity of this nation. And so we've come to cash this check, a check that will give us, upon demand the riches of freedom and the security of justice.[154]

He continued by speaking of his dream of a nation united in a freedom that rings on behalf of all persons. He closed his address by reciting his dream of universal unity in poetic form with a repeated exhortation of "Let freedom ring":

So let freedom ring from the prodigious
hills of New Hampshire.
Let freedom ring from the mighty
mountains of New York.
Let freedom ring from the heightening
Alleghenies of Pennsylvania.
Let freedom ring from the snow-capped
Rockies of Colorado.
Let freedom ring from the curvaceous
slopes of California.

But not only that.
Let freedom ring from the Stone
Mountain of Georgia.
Let freedom ring from the Lookout
Mountain of Tennessee.

Let freedom ring from every hill
and molehill of Mississippi,
from every mountainside,
let freedom ring.

And when we allow freedom to ring, when we let it ring from every village and every hamlet, from every state and city, we will be able to speed up that day when all of God's children – black men and white men, Jews and Gentiles, Catholics and Protestants – will be able to join hands and to sing in the words of the old Negro spiritual, "Free at last, free at last, thank God Almighty, we are free at last."[155]

Evidence of King's prophetic witness, and developing conception of the Christian love-ethic and call for peace with justice in the church and society is also found in his later views on the Vietnam War. He came to see a direct correlation between the Civil Rights movement in America and the War in Asia.[156] And he believed that he, as a preacher and leader, was called to give voice and witness on matters regarding war. He stated:

For those who ask the question, "Aren't you a Civil Rights leader?" and thereby mean to exclude me from the movement of peace, I have this further answer. In 1957 when a group of us formed the Southern Christian Leadership Conference, we chose as our motto: "To save the soul of America." We were convinced that we could not limit our vision to certain rights for black people, but instead affirmed the conviction that America would never be free or saved from itself unless the descendants of its slaves were loosed completely from the shackles they still were in. In a way we were agreeing with Langston Hughes, that black bard of Harlem, who had written earlier:

O yes,
I say it plain,
America never was America to me,
And yet I swear the oath –
America will be![157]

Regarding the War in Vietnam, King continued:

Now, it should be incandescently clear that no one who has any concern for the integrity and life of America today can ignore the present war. If America's soul becomes totally poisoned, part of the autopsy must read "Vietnam." It can never be saved so long as it destroys the deepest hopes of men the world over. So it is that those of us who are yet determined that America will be are led down the path of protest and dissent, working for the health of our land.

As if the weight of such a commitment to the life and health of America were not enough, another burden of responsibility was placed upon me in 1964; and I cannot forget that the Nobel Prize for Peace was also a commission – a commission to work harder than I had ever worked before for the "brotherhood of man." This is a calling that takes me beyond national allegiances, but even if it were not present I would yet have to live with the meaning of my commitment to the ministry of Jesus Christ. To me the relationship of this ministry to the making of peace is so obvious that I sometimes marvel at those who ask me why I am speaking against the war. Could it be that they do not know that the good news was meant for all men – for communist and capitalist, for their children and ours, for black and for white, for revolutionary and conservative? Have they forgotten that my ministry is in obedience to the one who loved his enemies so fully that he died for them? What then can I say to the "Viet Cong" or to Castro or to Mao as a faithful minister of this one? Can I threaten them with death or must I not share with them my life?[158]

### III.   *What might be appropriated?*

Martin Luther King, Jr. prophetically spoke and led within the context of the divine and moral imperative that the church and society share in seeking to eradicate racial hatred, economic oppression, social disintegration and global violence, and he advanced the appropriation of the Christian love-ethic as foundational for constructively moving toward the realization of the Beloved *Community*.

In the final analysis, his prophetic preaching and praxis offer insight for the contemporary church and society - and have implications and application in at least four principle areas: ***Call, Conviction, Courage and Commitment.***

## *Call*

King insisted that God's intent is for the human family to live in community as interrelated members. As an African American, he possessed a perspective on Christian faith that had been forged on the anvil of slavery, segregation and violent forms of racial oppression. In light of this, he consistently affirmed that all of humanity was bound together through their common creator. Hence, the fundamental tenets of love, forgiveness, reconciliation and prayer were to be the spiritual means of addressing extant forms of oppression, and building community.

King's sense of calling ultimately spawned his action. For instance, again, there is no indication that he had any personal intent, ambition or vocational/professional inclination to become the leader of the movement for racial and social justice in the South while in seminary or graduate school, but with the course and convergence of events within the context of his pastoral ministry at Dexter Avenue Baptist Church in Montgomery, Alabama - like biblical prophets - he came to the conclusion that it was indeed a part of his vocation and calling to become one of the prophetic public voices of the Civil Rights movement, first in Alabama, and then beyond.

Likewise, it is incumbent upon preachers and leaders today to clearly discern as to if and how they may be called by God to engage in prophetic public ministry and address the social concerns that may emerge. King's calling to peacemaking, justice-seeking and helping to realize the *Beloved Community* was seen throughout his ministry.

King captured the essence of his prophetic calling in a 1965 address where he recounted his entrance into the Civil rights movement. He spoke of having a call in the night. In January of 1956, when he was 27 years old and had been leading the Montgomery Bus Boycott, he received a threatening phone call at the parsonage of Dexter Avenue Baptist Church. This call was one among many that he would receive on any given night, threatening his life and the life of his family members. He intimated that this particular call touched a nerve and left him shaken. He sat at his kitchen table at midnight and prayed, "Lord, I'm down here trying to do what's right ... But ... I must confess ... I'm losing my courage." He explained what happened next: "I could hear an inner voice saying to me, 'Martin Luther, stand up for truth. Stand up for justice. Stand up for righteousness... and lo, I will be with you until the end of the age.'" [159]

According to Richard Lischer in *The Preacher King*, King here substantiated his prophetic vocation with an account of the very thing he had lacked as an apprentice preacher: a *call*, which in the African-American tradition "Is deemed to be more important than any kind of preparation."[160] Lischer shares the assertion of Israeli scholar Mechal Sobel who in *God Struck Me Dead* posited that the African-American experience of conversion follows a pattern of eight-steps: (1) The individual is brought before God. (2) God addresses the seeker by his very own "private name". (3) This signifies that God knows this person in the depth of the soul. (4) The person then "dies" and recounts the experience of his/her death. (5) The person is brought to the brink of hell. (6) God makes God's presence known to the saved person. (7) The person is sent back to earth by God. (8) The redeemed is free and will never again be confounded.[161]

Lischer concludes that with several modifications, King's "kitchen experience" in which the voice of God called him to a prophetic ministry, reproduces this traditional pattern.[162]

Over the course of his fourteen-year public ministry, it became clear that his praxis of prophetic ministry in the public sphere was ultimately rooted in a deep sense of a call by God. This imperative – this calling - was rooted and grounded in a divine commitment to advance the appropriation of the Christian love-ethic as foundational for constructively moving towards the realization of the *Beloved Community*.

### Conviction

For King, his sense of calling was acted upon within the context of his convictions. His convictions were largely rooted in his understanding of God and people. He believed that all persons were created by God with inherent worth, and that all people were therefore privy to the moral prerogatives of human dignity and social justice. He consistently affirmed what he deemed to be the *"somebodiness"* of all people regardless of race, class or other categories.[163]

King's demonstration of conviction mirrored that of other historic figures who have led prophetically. Here there is the reminder of the sentiments and acted out convictions of persons like:

- Frederick Douglas who, in his 19th century call for the abolition of slavery in America, intimated that progress never comes without struggle, and that "power concedes nothing without a demand".

- Fannie Lou Hamer, the Mississippi sharecropper who, in the 1950s and 60s, led the fight for voting rights for persons across the South, was one of the founders and leaders of the Mississippi Freedom Democratic Party, and reminded persons that progress comes through perseverance even when we are "sick and tired of being sick and tired".

- Mohandas K. Gandhi who in the midst of the revolutionary struggle for the freedom of the people of India reminded them that they had to become the change that they wished to see in the world.

- Dietrich Bonhoeffer, the German Lutheran pastor and theologian who engaged in the struggle to end

the atrocities of Hitler's Nazism, and reminded us
that Christian discipleship calls us to practice a
form of "costly grace".

- Desmond Tutu, who led the fight against South
African Apartheid, and its related racial/ethnic
atrocities.

In 1960, in an article published in the *Christian
Century*, titled "Pilgrimage to Nonviolence", King discussed
how he came to the conviction as to the necessity and
efficacy of nonviolence. He intimated:

> The experience of Montgomery did more to clarify
> my thinking on the question of nonviolence than all
> the books that I had read. As the days unfolded I
> became more and more convinced of the power of
> nonviolence. Living through the actual experience of
> protest, nonviolence became more than a method to
> which I gave intellectual assent; it became a
> commitment to a way of life.[164]

Ultimately, it was these convictions that led to King's
prophetic witness. Likewise, it is incumbent upon preachers
and leaders who might engage in the public square today to
be equally as clear about their convictions, and their belief
about God, God's people and God's will for peace with
justice.

## *Courage*

Courage serves as the measure of the human will to act on one's call and convictions – and to say and do what one believes to be true, just and right. Interestingly - among the books that King constantly carried with him as he travelled and provided leadership with the Civil Rights movement was Paul Tillich's *The Courage to Be.*

Concerning courage, Tillich wrote, "Few constructs are as useful for analysis of the human situation. Courage is an ethical reality, but it is rooted in the whole breadth of human existence and ultimately in the structure of being itself. It must be considered ontologically in order to be understood ethically."[165]

Tillich further intimated that the *courage to be* in its radical form is a key to an idea of God which transcends both mysticism and the person-to-person encounter... The *courage to be* in all its forms has, by itself, revelatory character. It shows the nature of being, it shows that the self-affirmation of being is an affirmation that overcomes negation.[166]

Courage to act on one's call and convictions means that one is willing to risk much of oneself - one's popularity, promotion and associations for the sake of the causes to which one feels called and convicted to prophetically address.

King's courage was born and bred out of the needs of the times in which he was called forth to provide prophetic voice and leadership. It is what Georg Wilhelm Friedrich

Hegel, and later those like King would refer to as the *zeitgeist,* or the spirt of the times, that spawned King and others into prophetic action. This is the courage that Queen Esther was summoned to in being an agent of protection and deliverance for her people. Amidst her perilous plight, and discerning if and how to act, her cousin Mordecai reminded her, *"Who knows—perhaps it was for a time like this that you became queen?"* (Esther 4:14) Howard Thurman alluded to such courage in in *Footprints of a Dream*:

> The movement of the Spirit of God in the hearts of men and women often calls them to act against the spirit of their times or causes them to anticipate a spirit which is yet in the making. In a moment of dedication they are given wisdom and courage to dare a deed that challenges and to kindle a hope that inspires.[167]

For King, it was such courage that would result in the refusal to give up against the insurmountable odds of racism and class oppression. He stated in *Where do We Go from Here?*:

> In any social revolution there are times when the tail winds of triumph and fulfillment favor us, and other times when strong headwinds of disappointments and setbacks beat against us relentlessly. We must not permit adverse winds to overwhelm us as we journey over life's mighty Atlantic; we must be sustained by our engines of courage in spite of the winds. This refusal to stop, this "courage to be", this

determination to go on "in spite of" is the hallmark of any great movement.[168]

## Commitment

In the aftermath of the 381-day Montgomery Bus Boycott in 1955-56, King made a statement that would become a signature of his prophetic witness when he said that "True peace in not merely the absence of tension, it is the presence of justice."[169] He would later state something that had been intimated by others before him, that "The arc of the moral universe is long, but it bends toward justice." These two statements speak clearly to his life-long commitments to promote racial equality, social justice and peace, his strivings to help eradicate what he deemed to be the "triplets of evil" - racism, poverty and war, and to help move the church and society toward becoming the *Beloved Community*.

Cornel West intimates that in 1967, King isolated himself from the demands of the Civil Rights movement, rented a house in Jamaica with no telephone, and labored over his final manuscript, *Where do We Go from Here?*. In the concluding chapter, King calls for the transcendence of race, nation and religion and for the embrace of a vision of the "World House" to eradicate at home and globally the triple evils of racism, poverty and militarism; to curb excessive militarism; and to use methods of nonviolence to fight for social justice.[170]

King wrote, "Among the moral imperatives of our time, we are challenged to work all over the world with the unshakable determination to wipe out the last vestiges of racism... Now as we stand two-thirds into this exciting period of history, we know full well that racism is still the hound of hell which dogs the tracks of our civilization."[171] His prophetic commitment to the end of his ministry and the tragic in end of his life in April 1968 was to work towards the eradication of the triplets of evil – racism, poverty and war.

It was out of his sense of *calling, conviction* and *courage* that King's *commitment* to do justice derived. Today, prophetic preaching and praxis likewise call for clear and consistent commitment in light of calling and conviction to speak truth to power, preach truth in love, to do justice, and the courage that can be mustered to carry this out.

Regarding his own commitments, on February, 4 1968, King preached "The Drum Major Instinct" from the pulpit of Ebenezer Baptist Church in Atlanta, Georgia, exactly two months before his assassination on April 4, 1968. Ironically, he told the congregation what he wanted to be shared in his eulogy. He stated, "I'd like somebody to mention that day that Martin Luther King Jr. tried to give his life serving others. I'd like for somebody to say that day that Martin Luther King Jr. tried to love somebody... Yes, if you want to, say that I was a drum major. Say that I was a drum major for justice. Say that I was a drum major for peace. I was a drum major for righteousness... But I just want to leave a committed life behind. And that is all I want to say. If I can help somebody as I pass along, if I can cheer somebody with a word or song, if I can show somebody he's traveling wrong, then my living will not be in vain."[172] (At the request of Mrs. Coretta Scott King, his widow, recorded words of this sermon by were played at his funeral.)

## CHAPTER FIVE

## THEOLOGICAL AND SOCIOLOGICAL DIMENSIONS OF THE BELOVED COMMUNITY

In *On God's Side*, Jim Wallis posits that *"The Beloved Community welcomes all tribes."*[173] Wallis shares a quote from Martin Luther King, Jr. that "our goal is to create a beloved community and this will require a qualitative change in our souls as well as a quantitative change in our lives."

Kenneth Smith and Ira Zepp, Jr. suggested that King's perspective on the Christian love-ethic provides critical insight into understanding his persistent search for the *"Beloved Community."*[174] Throughout his ministry, a recurring theme in his sermons, speeches and writings was what he called the *Beloved Community*. It was the ultimate goal for which he worked. For him, the *Beloved Community* was to be an integrated community in which persons of all races and creeds lived together harmoniously as sisters and brothers in peace. It was to be the kin-dom of God on earth. King stated, "I do not think of political power as an end. Neither do I think of economic power as an end. They are ingredients in the objective we seek in life. And I think that end, that objective, is a truly brotherly society, the creation of *Beloved Community*."[175]

*I.*    *Biblical and Theological Reflections on the Quest for the Beloved Community*

How might biblical and theological analysis speak to the quest for the *Beloved Community?* A careful reading of scripture clearly points to God's divine intent for all of humanity. The assertion that God has created all of humanity in God's image *(imago Dei)* was first recorded in scripture in the Book of Genesis (Gen. 1:26), and reminds us that God's purpose for humanity is rooted in our God-likeness. And it is in our God-likeness that we find our commonality in Christ.

Instances of the yearning towards the *Beloved Community* can be found throughout Scripture. It is seen in the prophet Isaiah's vision of the peaceable realm, where *wolves and lambs [would] lie down together* (Isa. 11:6). It is also seen in the prophet Micah's explication of what has come to be known as the Great Requirement, that we are to *"love kindness, do justice and walk humbly with God"* (Micah 6:8).

If the question is asked, should the body of Christ be divided by race, age, gender, and/or socio-economic status, many would clearly say 'no', and point to Galatians 3:26-29 that states:

> For in Christ Jesus you are all children of God through faith. As many of you as were baptized into Christ have clothed yourselves with Christ. There is no longer Jew or Greek, there is no longer

slave or free, there is no longer male and female; for all of you are one in Christ Jesus. And if you belong to Christ, then you are Abraham's offspring, heirs according to the promise.

God's will and desire for the church and the world is further evidenced in the words of the psalmist as found in Psalm 133:1-3:

How very good and pleasant it is when kindred live together in unity! It is like the precious oil on the head, running down upon the beard, on the beard of Aaron, running down over the collar of his robes. It is like the dew of Hermon, which falls on the mountains of Zion. For there the Lord ordained God's blessing, life forevermore.

This psalm speaks to the whole family of God, and reminds us of God's ideal that social barriers and religious walls of division be broken down, and that we unite with those who have been estranged from fellowship with God and God's people. It is important to first notice that the psalmist points to the blessing of not simply dwelling together, but *dwelling together in unity (community).* Certainly, the psalmist could have stopped by saying that it is blessed for persons to dwell together, but he went further to share that it's very good and pleasant in God's sight when persons *dwell together in unity.* *"For there the Lord ordained God's blessing, life forevermore" (Ps. 133:3).*

Howard Thurman was among those who shared King's vision and quest for the *Beloved Community*. In *The Search for Common Ground*, Thurman asserted that the search for common ground is a universal search among all of humanity. He stated that "A person is always threatened in one's very ground by a sense of isolation, by feeling oneself cut off from one's fellows. Yet, the person can never separate oneself from one's fellows, for mutual interdependence is characteristic of all life."[176] Thus, for Thurman, like King, this common, universal quest and search for common ground has teleological implications, as it essentially provides the framework for the meaning of life itself.

This quest for unity is tied to the quest for justice, and is ultimately tied to the quest for understanding what it means to be human. In her book *Ferguson and Faith, Sparking Leadership and Awakening Community*, Leah Gunning Francis intimated that "The fight for justice… is the fight to be seen and valued as human beings "just as you are"- not in a prescribed way that renders you acceptable so long as you fit a particular mold, but in an authentic way that makes room for each person to be able to be fully him – or herself."[177]

## II.    *The Beloved Community amidst Human Diversity*

In the twenty-first century, one of the critical challenges for the churches and society relates to how to most faithfully, effectively and compassionately address the complex social, economic and political dilemmas that exist in ways that will best facilitate the building of authentic, sustained community. Racism, classism, militarism, sexism, politicism, denominationalism and tribalism pervade society and churches, and serve to create and perpetuate tremendous barriers among people, and hindrances to community.

At the heart of the quest for the *Beloved Community* is seeing how the church has in the past, and discovering how it might in the future, be equipped to affirm both its universality (catholicity and ecumenism) and its inclusiveness (unity) in light of the diversity among people. Though, in America, many Southern and Eastern European ethnic groups have assimilated into Anglo-American culture, they have done so at a great cost to themselves, in terms of a sense of personal identity and worth, and to society as a whole. Still, in the past, white Europeans could assimilate while non-white ethnic groups could not. At best, ethnic minority groups could only imitate the dominant culture, but never really merge into it. For this reason, "ethnicity" has come to refer to those ethnic groups which in reality are "unmeltable" – African Americans, Hispanic Americans, Native Americans and Asian Americans. Indeed, the increasing "rediscovery" of ethnicity by whites of Southern and Eastern European ancestry has been spearheaded by efforts of the "unmeltable" ethnic groups to rediscover their identities. Also, it has been the so-called ethnic minority groups that have forced the growing realization among Anglo-Americans that they too are an ethnic group – one culture among many, rather than *the* culture.[178] The discovery of and living into the diversity that comprises society is enhanced through honest and open dialogue and engagement with those of other cultures – with the constant realization that God is the creator of all peoples and cultures.

As the Body of Christ, the church is to serve as an integrative bridge across the divides of the many societal entities with which it relates. One way that this might be accomplished is by striving towards racial and cultural pluralism, which reflects the diversity among peoples. A comprehension and appropriation of pluralism is an important asset in the movement towards the *Beloved Community*.[179] The issue, therefore, remains how to discover common ground among persons from different cultural, socioeconomic, political, racial and religious backgrounds.

The recognition and valuation of human diversity entails several presumptions about God the creator, and humanity that has been created by God. In his book, *Christian Moral Judgment*, ethicist J. Phillip Wogaman refers to this as the method of positive presumption.[180] According to Wogaman, we presume: (1) *The goodness of created existence.* God created humanity (all humans) in goodness and wholeness. God's divine intention for created humanity is goodness and wholeness (shalom). (2) *The value of human life.* In each human being there is sacred and infinite worth as a result of humanity's creation in God's image (*imago Dei*). (3) *The unity of the human family.* Humans have not been created to live in a vacuum, but in community with one another. Because of our creation by the same God, we are all interconnected and interrelated. (4) *The equality of all persons in God.* As God has created all persons in the image of God, and as there is unity among humans in God, there is also equality among all human beings. Wogaman asserts that amidst human diversity, there must be an affirmation of the intrinsic value and equality of all persons.

Henry Mitchell and Nicholas Cooper-Lewter, in *Soul Theology: The Heart of American Black Culture,* point out that equality is not merely political rhetoric; it involves God's justice expressed impartially.[181] With regard to equality, they state:

> Either God regards all persons as intrinsically equal, or (God) is the unjust author of inequity, the very Creator of the oppressions suffered by persons and groups at the bottom of the social and economic system. As easy as it may be to practice inequality, the American dream will not permit it to be approved by the Creator...The founders of this nation attributed their egalitarian dogma to the very mind of God, and so Americans have believed ever since.
>
> This equality is not to be mistaken for uniformity, however. Americans come in different sizes and shapes. They have various levels of giftedness, in a further diversified spectrum of specialties. They represent a fantastic variety of colors and cultures, from every corner of the earth, to say nothing of the profusion of personality patterns. Still, before the law, they are all equal in standing. Few affirmations have more sweeping consequences psychologically and spiritually, as well as legally, and few are so

inadequately articulated, especially in America's circle of power. The pluralism of the dream is far better understood today than ever, but the drift toward the tyranny of single-group supremacy and enforced uniformity is always present.[182]

The familiar Negro spiritual speaks to the notion of the equality that intrinsically exists among persons:

*The fare is cheap, and all can ride,*
*the rich and the poor are there.*
*No second class aboard this train,*
*no difference in the fare.*
*Oh, get on board, little children,*
*get on board, little children,*
*Get on board, little children,*
*there room for many a 'more.*[183]

### III.   UBUNTU Theology and the Quest for the Beloved Community

Closely aligned with the concept of the *Beloved Community* is the Zulu concept, *Ubuntu*. Anglican Archbishop Desmond Tutu, in his nonviolent battle against Apartheid in South Africa, rallied around the concept of *Ubuntu*, "I am what I am because of who we all are, and therefore, because of who we are, I am." Jim Wallis points to the *Ubuntu* theology of Tutu as being a sign of hope for a movement towards appropriating (and re-appropriating) the

*Beloved Community* in the 21$^{st}$ century.[184] A quote from Tutu emphasizes the criticality of *Ubuntu*, "You might have much of the world's riches, and might have a portion of authority, but if you have no *Ubuntu*, you do not amount to much."

*Ubuntu* speaks to the very quality of being human, affirms the fundamental humanness of all persons, and asserts the support that we must afford each other if we are to be all that God calls us to be. According to sociolinguist Buntu Mfentana, *Ubuntu* "runs through the veins of Africans." *Ubuntu* speaks to the humanity that is imbedded in all persons by virtue of the fact that we are all human. Lente-Louis Louw in *Valuing Diversity* elaborates and states that the quality of being human for Africans is embodied in the oft-repeated proverb, "A person is a person through other people."[185]

It essentially insists that "If I diminish you, I diminish myself".[186] And it pushes back against words and actions that harm bodies and souls. As Tutu further asserts:

> "… anger, resentment, a lust for revenge, even the aggressive competitiveness that rules so much of the contemporary world, corrodes and jeopardizes our harmony. *Ubuntu* points out that those who seek to destroy and dehumanize are also victims – victims, usually of a pervading ethos, be it political ideology, an economic system, or a distorted religious conviction. Consequently, they are as much dehumanized as those on whom they trample.[187]

*Ubuntu,* thus binds persons together as the human family, and manifests itself through various human acts, clearly visible in social, political and economic situations, as well as among family and other forms of community. A commitment to the realization of *Ubuntu* offers hope for the world in which we live.

It essentially speaks to the quest for the *Beloved Community.* Community – common ground – by its very nature - is integrative; it speaks to a "common unity" among us. Forms of disintegration, disunity and disembodiment are, therefore, to be understood as being antithetical to the common good, community and to the will of God. The *Beloved Community* includes persons of different races, genders, ages, religions, cultures, viewpoints, lifestyles and stages of development - and serves – as *Ubuntu* insists - to synergistically integrate persons into a whole that is greater – more actualized and dynamic – than the sum of its parts.

### IV. The Beloved Community and Culture

Eric H. F. Law, in *The Bush Was Burning but Not Consumed,* defines culture as learned values, beliefs, perceptions, assumptions, patterns and practices – both conscious and unconscious – that enable (persons and groups) to perceive, interpret, evaluate and respond to life and the world. Culture… is not limited to race and ethnicity, even though for many (persons) race and ethnicity constitute the major aspects of one's cultural identity and makeup. Other components that contribute to a person's culture can include gender, age, physical ability, sexual orientation, economic status, religion, marital status, education, community, geography, work, family structure, and individual interests and experiences.[188]

Culture can thus be understood as embodied in the language, symbols, music, dress, *mores,* customs and traditions that serve as the source of validity, vitality and perpetuity for a group of people. In the valuation of cultures, persons in the church and society are called to understand the contributions that existing cultures make to the whole body of Christ. In two lectures given at the Greenfield Center for Human Relations at the University of Pennsylvania in 1954, which was expanded into a volume entitled *Cultural Pluralism and the American Idea,* Horace Kallen offered what has become a classic analysis of culture:

> A living culture is a changing culture; and it is… not an auctioneer's storage house or an archaeological dump of fragments, fossils and ruins, because of the transactions wherewith living, altering individuals' old thoughts and things while laboring to preserve them and to produce new. Cultures live and grow in and through the individual, and their vitality is a function of individual diversities of interests and associations. Pluralism is the *sine qua non* of their persistence and prosperous growth. But not the absolutist pluralism which the concept of the unaltering and inalterable Monad discloses. On the contrary, the *sine qua non* is fluid, relational pluralism which the living individual encounters in the transactions wherewith he constructs his personal

history moving out of groups and into groups, engaging in open or hidden communion with societies of his fellows, every one different from the others, and all teamed together, and struggling to provide and maintain the common means which nourish, assure and enhance the different, and often competing, values they differently cherish.[189]

The quest for the *Beloved Community* affirms the value of the diverse cultures of which persons are a part. Christian evangelist E. Stanley Jones, in his work with Mohandas Gandhi and the people of India, suggested that persons from diverse cultures could indeed engage in authentic community-building. But the objective in cross-cultural contexts should not be to change persons' cultural orientation, or to impose one's own culture upon others, but to seek to understand and value other persons.[190]

When the imposition of culture upon indigenous peoples has occurred, often in the name of religion, cultures have often fallen apart. Noted Nigerian author Chinua Achebe referred to this as "things falling apart."[191] Cultures, communities, families and individuals are affected when there is insensitivity and a lack of understanding and valuation of other cultures and peoples.

Jean Marc Ela, in *My Faith as An African,* spoke to the pervasive nature of culture, particularly in relation to the gospel of Christ. Ela pointed out that evangelizing people shaped by a certain culture must go hand in hand with their struggle for development in all aspects of their lives. The hope for a New World that is built in the framework of justice, peace and freedom is the heart of the Christian message.[192] According to Ela, this is the starting point for a radical critique of all that is happening before us in terms of intercultural engagement.

Any notion of Christ as Liberator, and a gospel that seeks to promote peace and to liberate those who find themselves in the bonds of injustice and oppression, operates from the ground up – at the existential point of cultural context – the places and realities where persons currently find themselves.

According to cognitive theorists in cultural anthropology, culture is a knowledge system existing in people's minds that they use to govern behavior. It is not the behavior itself that governs culture, but the cognitive systems of ideas, values and beliefs that people must know to generate behavior acceptable to the cultural group.[193]

The valuation of and openness towards diverse cultures can also be understood within the context of *inculturation* or *contextualization*. The implications here are renewed understandings of the church and the church's ministry in the world. They suggest "incarnation" and "insertion", and the impossibility of separating a people's culture and religious habits; and they do so precisely because they recognize that wherever we go, our culture goes with us. The processes of *inculturation* and *contextualization* seek to move persons towards *interculturation* and *multiculturation*. This begins at the point of the *ethnocentricity* of individuals and communities who – through exposure to cultures other than their own - begin to gain an *ethnorelative* awareness of aspects of the other's culture within the context of their own *ethnocentric* perspective. Through this heightened awareness, persons begin to gain a more profound understanding of the differences and similarities of other cultures, which leads eventually to a sense of valuation. In valuation, one gains a respect and appreciation for the importance of "other" cultures to their own spirituality and growth – thus resulting in the eventual selective adoption of some aspects of other cultures into one's own sense of being.[194]

Movement towards a realization of the *Beloved Community* involves an understanding and appreciation of the nuances of culture, which is rooted in self-awareness as well as the broader awareness of, and sensitivity to, the "other" that becomes a part of one's reality over time. This process of *interculturation/multiculturation* is critical to the development of the *Beloved Community*.

## V. The Beloved Community and the Church's Mission and Ministry

The Church is the means by which the ministry of Jesus Christ as the kin-dom of God is continuously carried forth into the world. Through its various means of serving the world, the church is the redemptive bridge between God and all humanity. It is God working in and through persons, as God continues through Christ to reconcile the world unto Godself. As Paul intimated, "God was in Christ reconciling the world to Godself" (2 Corinthians 5:17-18).

The model of ministry as taught to the world by Christ is one of inclusive, universal witness and service. Christ's ministry was directed particularly towards the marginalized: those persons with needs that various societal institutions had failed to address. By feeding the hungry, clothing the naked and healing those who suffered, Christ demonstrated that the commonality of human strengths and weaknesses far transcends the many differences that tend to divide persons.

Throughout his ministry, Jesus demonstrated that there is to be an ongoing relationship between the church and the world. The mission of the church is thus to be carried out in and with the world on behalf of God from whom all ministry originates, through whom it flows, and to whom it belongs.

The church's active participation in the world can be translated as its mission. This mission is to be seen, first and foremost, as the mission of God (*missio Dei*). It has its origins in divine grace, which is ultimately witnessed to in the Christian community by God's unconditional love (*agape*) in sending Jesus into a troubled world. It is this *missio Dei*, derived out of grace, that is the motivation, context and content of the church's ministry in, with and for the world. The church exists to exemplify and embody God's grace amidst the suffering and violence extant throughout the world. Even in brokenness, God's justice and mercy are intended to be evident in and through the church.

In the Church's quest to become the emblem of the *Beloved Community*, it endeavors to model the ministry of

Christ - a ministry of unconditional love, compassion, justice, redemption and reconciliation – through which Jesus sought to address the particular spiritual and social concerns among those whom he encountered. To engage in a ministry of community-building is to participate in the *missio Dei,* and to live a life in radical witness of and service to Christ. As Christ offers peace with justice to the world, the Church is likewise called to share in ministries of peace and justice.

### VI. The Beloved Community as a Means and Ends of Spiritual and Social Transformation

The *Beloved Community* as a vision of hope is ultimately a call and commitment to seek spiritual and social transformation, for the sake of Christ, of the world in which we live. As such, it is a forceful challenge to rise above ourselves – our personal differences and agendas - and live according to God's divine plan. The Psalmist's exhortation to *"turn from evil and do good, seek peace and pursue it"* (Psalm 34:14) has all the urgency and realism of the law of love and, as such, has the transforming power to take us beyond whatever we thought possible. Paul encouraged Christians in Rome to *"be not conformed to the world, but be transformed by the renewing of your minds" (Romans 12:1).* In order to be transformed, we must first be attuned to our weaknesses and vulnerabilities, and thus our shared needs for individual and communal change.

The peacefulness that so characterizes our age has its roots in self-deception and in a neurosis stemming from repressed truth.[195] These manifest themselves in our prejudices and misunderstandings, often unconscious, which become embedded in our thought patterns and language, and ultimately in our behaviors.

Theologian Dorothee Solle, in *Thinking about God*, wrote of the relationship of righteousness to peace and social transformation:

> The foundation of peace is righteousness. *"Grace and truth meet each other, righteousness and peace kiss each other"* (Psalm 85:10). The goal is the state in which God has destroyed the chariots and put an end to aggression. Without social justice, without righteousness, there is no peace. According to the prophets the criterion is the rights of those without rights – for example women and orphans, who have no male advocate. The lowest class is made the criterion for the prosperity of all: those who have been most deprived of their rights, who have the least to say, who not only have no money but also no advocate, no connections, who cannot even go to the authorities because they do not know what they can claim – they are the criterion for what righteousness really is.[196]

The unbridled pursuit of material achievement, coupled with a sense of self-righteousness and exaggerated self-interest, can make us blind to higher values and to the real needs of others. Such exaggerated self-interest can result in the perpetuation of institutionalized injustice and violent conflict. Critical self-awareness will help us avoid blind utilitarianism and unhealthy self-interest, which confuse human values with materialism, and freedom with exploitation.

At the heart of the prophet Amos' challenge and vision to *"let justice roll down as waters, and righteousness as an ever-flowing stream"* (Amos 5:24) is the hope of transformation of persons and communities. There can be no hopeful enterprise of the *Beloved Community* if there is not an awareness of the social distortions in our midst, and if we do not keep watch over our motives and intentions. We must be willing to critique the genuineness of our love and commitments. The hope of peace with justice demands that we become critically conscious of the interests and motives that guide our actions.

The ultimate objective of peacemaking and community-building is the spiritual and social transformation of persons and institutions. This is the teleological concern that is before us. Hope says to us that it is therefore insufficient to simply maintain the present condition, plight and status quo. The objective is to effect positive and progressive change, and to help persons experience the life-transforming, all-enveloping presence and love of God which will enable and empower communities to stretch beyond the comfort zones of human circumstances. Hope lies in the prospect of discovering a creative catalyst that will energize humanity's quest to transform and be transformed. As peace with justice is realized, lives and relationships are eventually changed to reflect the reality of *shalom* – the wholeness, well-being, and salvation that is the essence of the *Beloved Community*.

## CHAPTER SIX

## *MARTIN LUTHER KING, JR.,*
## *THE CHRISTIAN LOVE-ETHIC AND*
## *NONVIOLENCE*


Martin Luther King, Jr.'s perspective on the Christian love-ethic was perhaps most clearly explicated in his sermon entitled, "Loving Your Enemies."[197] The sermon was based on Jesus' admonition to his disciples in Matthew 5:43-45:

> *"You have heard that it was said, 'You shall love your neighbor, and hate your enemy.' But I say to you, love your enemies, and pray for those who persecute you, so that you may be children of your Father which is in heaven; for he makes his sun rise on the evil and the good, and sends rain on the righteous and on the unrighteous."*

In the sermon, King asserted that probably no admonition of Jesus has been more difficult to follow than the command to "love your enemies." With regard to the difficulty found here, King stated:

Some men have sincerely felt its actual practice is not possible. It is easy, they say, to

> love those who love you, but how can one love those who openly and insidiously seek to defeat you? Others, like Nietzsche, contend that Jesus' exhortation to love one's enemies is testimony to the fact that the Christian ethic is designed for the weak

and cowardly, and not for the strong and courageous. Jesus, they say, is an impractical idealist.[198]

Loving one's enemies, or those who may act with hatred and malice, or those with whom one might disagree and differ socially, politically, economically, religiously, or even morally, is indeed possible, according to King. Loving one's enemies is not optional, but is essential to living out what it means to be Christian. He offered a model for how one is to love an enemy.[199] First, King posited, *the capacity to forgive must be developed.* He who is devoid of the power to forgive is devoid of the power to love. It is impossible even to begin the act of loving one's enemies without the prior acceptance of the necessity, over and over again, of forgiving those who inflict evil and injury upon us. It is also necessary to realize that the forgiving act must always be initiated by the person who has been wronged, the victim of some great hurt, the recipient of some tortuous injustice, the absorber of some terrible act of oppression.

Second, *it must be recognized that the evil deed of the enemy-neighbor, that thing that hurts, never quite expresses all that he is.* An element of goodness may be found in even the worst enemy. According to King, each of us is something of a schizophrenic personality, tragically divided against ourselves. "A persistent civil war rages within all our lives," he said. "Something within us causes us to lament with Ovid, the Latin poet, "I see and approve of better things, but follow worse," or to agree with Plato that human personality is like a charioteer having two headstrong horses, each wanting to go in a different direction, or to repeat the Apostle Paul, "The good that I would I do not; but the evil which I would not, that I do."

Third, *there must be no effort to defeat or humiliate the enemy, but to win his friendship and understanding.* King said: "At times we are able to humiliate our worst enemy. Inevitably, his weak moments come and we are able to thrust inside the spear of defeat. But this we must not do. Every word and deed must contribute to an understanding with the enemy and release those vast reservoirs of goodwill which have been blocked by impenetrable walls of hate."

He concluded by defining love (*agape*) as the means by which we overcome the propensity towards hatred and humiliation:

> *Agape* is the love of God operating in the human heart. When we rise to love on the *agape* level, we rise to the position of loving the person who does the evil deed, while hating the deed which the person does.[200]

William Shannon, in *Seeds of Peace,* offered a perspective on the nature of unconditional love:

> Unconditional love is love that makes demands on oneself more than on the other. It is a love that brooks no "if" clauses. It does not say: "I love you, if you do this or that." Instead it says: "I love you regardless of what you do or say. I love you because, no matter what you say or do, you are the icon, the image of God. Precisely because I love you, I will

confront you with the truth and challenge you with its demands. But I will also be a listener. I will try to hear what you are saying. For I realize that I do not possess all the truth; and there may well be things you have to say to me that I need to hear. But regardless of how much we may differ, I shall try always to remember the contemplative vision: that you and I are one in God. That oneness exists at a level of perception that perhaps we do not often enough achieve. But I know in faith that that oneness is a reality. And since we are one, I must love you as my other self. There can be no strings attached to my love for you."[201]

*Agape* is not a weak, passive love. It is love in action. It seeks to preserve, create and sustain community. It is insistent on community even when one seeks to break it. *Agape* entails a willingness to go to any length to build community where it does not exist, and restore community when it is broken. It does not stop at the first mile, but it goes the second mile to build and restore community. It is a willingness to forgive, not seven times, but seventy times seven.

The Cross is the eternal and divine expression of *agape,* and shows the length to which God will go in order to restore broken humanity and community. Jesus reminded persons of his day of this when he stated, *"For God so loved the world, that God sent God's only begotten son, so that whoever believes in him will not perish, but have eternal life"* (John 3:16). And Paul further stated that, *"God demonstrates God's love toward us, in that while we were sinners, Christ died for us"* (Romans 5:8). The Resurrection of Christ is a sign of God's triumph over hatred and all forces that seek to break community. The Holy Spirit is the continuing community-creating and sustaining reality that moves through history. Those who work against community are working against the whole of God's creation and love, and the perichoresis of who God is in divine love - as Creator, Savior and Sustainer.

Therefore, if the response to hate is reciprocal hate, then there is nothing but intensification of the cleavage in broken community. If hate is met with hate, persons become depersonalized and desensitized because creation is so designed such that human personality can only be fulfilled in the context of community. Booker T. Washington once said: "Let no man pull you so low he brings you to the point of working against community; he drags you to the point of defying creation, and therefore becoming depersonalized."[202]

King asserted that *agape* is recognition of the fact that all life is interrelated, and thus his fundamental belief that all people are a part of God's family. This profound understanding of faith highlighted the God-giftedness of all persons, the equality that is inherent in all humanity, and the unending hope that society – amidst the inexhaustible power of this God-giftedness, and despite the existential and communal fallenness that is evidenced in the perpetuation of the race line and other forms of human division – possesses the grace, if not yet the will, to overcome forms of division.

## Philosophy of Nonviolence

Owing to the eloquence of King's words, it is easy to lose sight of his singular vision of nonviolent social resistance as a means of realizing the *Beloved Community*. It is critical not to lose sight of his prophetic vision and his understanding of Christian faith, which led him to stand up against the most dominant and insipid social realities of his day – racism, classism/poverty and militarism.

King's theological project to link his conception of God-giftedness – as rooted in his early intellectual and spiritual development - to dialectical Christian praxis led him to call the Christian community and the broader world to a form of sacrificial witness that would move persons of all races and nationalities beyond existing paradigms of ritual, theology and partisan persuasion, and towards authentic community. If the church were to be the church, it would engage in a witness that would prophetically and progressively bring its spiritual, social, economic and political resources to bear in ways that would be truly transforming, liberating, reconciling and redeeming.

In as much as nonviolence was the foundation that brought about social and political change, King viewed nonviolence as a process that would ultimately lead to spiritual and social transformation, and the realization of the *Beloved Community*. For him, nonviolence was not an end in itself – but a means for the church and society to appropriate community; and for him nonviolence, again, was a philosophy and praxis that clearly had its roots in the black churches. In a speech to the National Conference on Religion and Race in 1963, King said:

> I am happy to say that the nonviolent movement in America has come not from secular forces but from the heart of the Negro church... The great principles of love and justice which stand at the center of the nonviolent movement are deeply rooted in our Judeo-Christian heritage. [203]

Historian Lerone Bennett suggested that King and his thinking on the Christian love-ethic and nonviolence was greatly influenced by Howard Thurman. Bennett intimated that when he went to Montgomery, Alabama, shortly after the beginning of the Montgomery Bus Boycott, he was not at all surprised to find King reading not Mohandas Gandhi, but Howard Thurman.[204] In his book, *America's Original Sin: Racism, White Privilege and the Bridge to a New America,* Jim Wallis points out that one of the books that King carried with him whenever he traveled was Thurman's *Jesus and the Disinherited.*[205]

The 1955-56 Montgomery Bus Boycott captured the attention and support of the nation and much of the world. It served as the impetus for King's theo-praxis of nonviolent social resistance. What had begun as a demonstration for a better form of segregation (first-come/first-serve seating on city buses) developed under his skillful and charismatic leadership into a holy cause. What was aimed at a week's duration stretched into 381 days of "tired feet and rested souls."

*C. Anthony Hunt*

Jim Crow was very much alive in the Deep South in the 1950s, but major surgery was performed on the dis-ease of racism in Montgomery. At the end of the bus boycott, almost half of Black America had been involved in one way or another. The period ushered in by the Montgomery bus protest is of enormous significance. There is very little question that Montgomery opened the door to a period of the most frenetic activity in the history of race relations in America. Martin Luther King, Jr., a Black Brahmin of well-to-do parentage, credentialed at Boston University, young, gifted, and a Black preacher, introduced the modern techniques of Gandhi, wrapped up in the religion and morality of the folk churches. King's nonviolent program of attack against an old enemy (segregation) on a scale of mass involvement, constructively channeled the bitter and frustrated energies of a people too often betrayed.[206]

**Principles of Nonviolence**

Nonviolence played a critical role in King's thinking and practice throughout the Montgomery Movement, and remained integral to his thought and praxis through the remainder of his 14-year public ministry. This philosophy had several elements that he would continue to develop, refine and deploy throughout his life, and which were expressed in a set of principles which he outlined in his first book *Stride toward Freedom* in 1958.[207] An analysis of King's thinking indicates six general characteristics of the practice of nonviolent resistance as a means of protest and community-building.

First, according to King, *it must be emphasized that nonviolent resistance is not a method for passive cowards.* Nonviolent resistance was conceived by him and those who were a part of the Civil Rights movement as a method of active resistance. Persons were not to engage in nonviolent resistance because they were afraid or merely because of a lack of the instruments of violence. Mohandas Gandhi often said that if cowardice is the only alternative to violence, it is better to fight. He made this statement conscious of the fact that there is always another alternative to violence. Nonviolence is ultimately the way of the strong person. It is not a method of stagnant passivity, weakness or fear. The phrase "passive resistance" is often used in conjunction with nonviolent resistance. But a distinction should be made between "passive resistance" and nonviolent direct action, in that the notion of "passive resistance" gives the impression of a lack of active involvement in which the resister quietly and passively accepts evil. While in nonviolent direct action, the resister is passive in the sense that he or she is not physically aggressive towards the opponent, the resister's mind and emotions are always active, constantly seeking to persuade their opponent of the evil that is present. The method is passive physically, but strongly active spiritually, morally, mentally and intellectually. It is not passive nonresistance to evil, it is active nonviolent resistance to evil.

A second basic characteristic of nonviolent resistance, according to King, is that *it does not seek to defeat or humiliate the opponent, but to win his friendship and understanding.* In this regard, he stated:

> The nonviolent resister most often expresses his protest through non-cooperation or boycotts, but he realizes that these are not ends themselves; they are merely means to awaken a sense of moral shame in the opponent. The end is redemption and reconciliation. The aftermath of nonviolence is the creation of *Beloved Community*, while the aftermath of violence is tragic bitterness.

When the Montgomery Bus Boycott ended, King spoke at a victory rally on December 23, 1956. He spoke words of reconciliation and hope for the future. He pointed out that the goal of the bus boycott had not been to defeat other persons, but to awaken the conscience of others to challenge the false sense of superiority that persons might harbor. Now that victory had been achieved, he said, it was time for reconciliation. "The end is reconciliation; the end is the creation of *Beloved Community*."

The *Beloved Community* – the loving community of peace, justice and equality - can only be attained by loving means. Community cannot be built on the tools of hatred. Nonviolence responds in a caring way to the perpetrator of violence. It announces that the well-being of the individuals involved is of ultimate concern. It moves the level of confrontation to a higher spiritual plane. Instead of merely defeating one's offender physically or psychologically, one begins to create the climate for love to be a force, which has to be dealt with within the context of relationships and fellowship. The presence of loving care and concern introduces new possibilities for reconciliation and community. Only nonviolence permits love to enter conflict creatively and address the prevailing spiritual ills of separation, fear and hatred.

A third characteristic of this nonviolent method is that *the attack is directed against forces of evil rather than against persons who happen to be doing evil.* Regarding this distinction, King pointed out:

> It is evil that the nonviolent resister seeks to defeat, not the persons who are the perpetrators of evil. If one is opposing racial injustice, the nonviolent resister has the vision to see that the basic tension is not between the persons of different races.

He continued by pointing out:

> As I like to say to the people of Montgomery: "The tension in this city is not between white people and Negro people. The tension is, at bottom, between justice and injustice, between the forces of light and the forces of darkness. And if there is victory, it will not be merely for fifty thousand Negroes, but a victory for justice and the forces of light. We are out to defeat injustice and not white persons who may be unjust."

A fourth characteristic of nonviolent resistance is *a willingness to accept suffering without retaliation, to accept blows from the opponent without striking back.* Here, King referred to the thinking of Mohandas Gandhi to make his point about the suffering of the resister:

> Gandhi said to his countrymen, "Rivers of blood may have to flow before we gain freedom, but it must be our blood." The nonviolent resister is willing to accept violence if necessary, but never to inflict it. He does not seek to dodge jail if going to jail is necessary to meet the objectives of social change through nonviolence.

The nonviolent resister's justification for this is found in the notion that unearned suffering is redemptive. The nonviolent resister posits that suffering has tremendous educational and transformational possibilities. Gandhi said:

> Things of fundamental importance to people are not secured by reason alone, but have to be purchased with their suffering.... Suffering is infinitely more powerful than the law of the jungle for converting the opponent and opening his ears which are otherwise shut to the voice of reason.

In an article in the *Christian Century* in 1960, entitled "Suffering and Faith", King reflected further upon the matter of the redemptive and transformational qualities of suffering:[208]

> Some of my personal sufferings over the last few years have also served to shape my thinking. I always hesitate to mention these experiences for fear of conveying the wrong impression. A person who

constantly calls attention to his trials and sufferings is in danger of developing a martyr complex and of making others feel that he is consciously seeking sympathy. It is possible for one to be self-centered in his self-denial, and self-righteous in his self-sacrifice. So I am always reluctant to refer to my personal sacrifices. But I feel somewhat justified in mentioning them in this article because of the influence they have had in shaping my thinking.

Due to my involvement in the struggle for the freedom of my people, I have known very few quiet days in the last few years. I have been arrested five times and put in Alabama jails. My home has been bombed twice. A day seldom passes that my family and I are not the recipients of threats of death. I have been the victim of a near-fatal stabbing. So in a real sense I have been battered by the storms of persecution. I must admit that at times I have felt that I could no longer bear such a heavy burden, and have been tempted to retreat to a more quiet and serene life. But every time such a temptation appeared, something came to strengthen and sustain my determination. I have learned now that the Master's burden is light precisely when we take his yoke upon us.

My personal trials have also taught me the value of unmerited suffering. As my sufferings mounted I soon realized that there were two ways that I could respond to my situation: either to react with bitterness or seek to transform the suffering into a creative force. I decided to follow the latter course. Recognizing the necessity of suffering, I have tried to make of it a virtue. If only to save myself from bitterness, I have attempted to see my personal ordeals as an opportunity to transform myself and heal the people involved in the tragic situation, which now obtains. I have lived these last few years with the conviction that unearned suffering is redemptive.

King persistently sought to articulate a theodicy (rationale for the justice of God and coherency of the problem of evil) which gave coherency to the suffering and injustices inflicted upon oppressed and marginalized persons. He also sought to make a clear connection between spirituality and suffering. Gustavo Gutierrez speaks of the challenge of making this connection in *On Job: God-talk and the Suffering of the Innocent:*

> This then is the question: Are suffering human beings able to enter into an authentic relationship with God and find a correct way of speaking about God? If the answer is yes, then it will be a priori possible to do the same in other human situations. But if the answer is no, then it will be irrelevant that persons living in less profound and challenging situations "appear" to accept the gratuitousness of God's love and claim to practice a disinterested religion. Human suffering is the harsh, demanding ground on which the wager about talk of God is

made; it is also that which ensures that the wager has universal applicability.[209]

In historical context and philosophical perspective, suffering may be viewed in dialectical terms. Perhaps the most perpetual dilemma for people of faith has been seeking to address a perennial question, "Why do bad things happen to good people?" There are several theological views that have been posited to address this dilemma. Suffering might be seen as a path towards spiritual growth. Through suffering, the thinking here is that persons may gain spiritual refinement. Suffering might also be understood eschatologically as preparation for a "reward" to be received in the next world. Suffering might also be viewed within the context of vicarious suffering (atonement) where one suffers sacrificially for the benefit of others for some greater cause. Christ's suffering on the Cross for the redemption of humanity's sins is an example of the atonement theory of suffering.

There also have been a number of philosophical perspectives that speak to the matter of suffering among persons of faith. The philosophic dilemma seems to derive essentially from the problem of evil, and the question, "If God is all-powerful and all-loving, then why and how is there suffering and injustice in the world?" Given the existence of suffering and evil, one might then be led to question the existence of God, or at the very least, to question the all-powerful, all-loving nature of God. The conclusion here may be that evil, injustice and suffering may mean the very absence of God.

Austrian psychologist Viktor Frankl sought to address the matter of unmerited, unavoidable suffering within the context of his experiences during the Jewish Holocaust of the early-20th century. In *Man's Search for Meaning,* he posited that we can discover meaning in life by the attitude we take towards unavoidable suffering. With regard to this, Frankl offered:

> We must never forget that we may also find meaning in life even when confronted with a hopeless situation, when facing a fate that cannot be changed. For what then matters is to bear witness to the uniquely human potential at its best, which is to transform a personal tragedy into triumph, to turn one's predicament into a human achievement. When we are no longer able to change a situation – just think of an incurable disease such as inoperable cancer – we are challenged to change ourselves... In some ways, suffering ceases to be suffering at the moment that it finds meaning, such as the meaning of sacrifice.[210]

Elie Wiesel in his book entitled, *Night,* wrote of the experience of the Holocaust for him and his father, and like Frankl sought to bring coherency and meaning to the problem of human suffering and evil.[211] Wiesel depicted night as embodying in its most hopeful dimension, a transition from darkness to light, filled with the promise of the beginning of a new day. But he wanted to show that there is too often a certain tragic irony and finality of the night that results in everything coming to an end. About

*Night*, Wiesel wrote, "I wanted to show the end, the finality of the event. Everything came to an end – man, history, life and meaning. There was nothing left."

In April 2002, Wiesel again reflected on his experiences during the Holocaust and shared:

> "People say occasionally that there must be light at the end of the tunnel, but I believe in those times there was light in the tunnel. In a strange way there was courage in the ghetto, and there was hope, human hope, in the death camps. Simply an anonymous prisoner giving a piece of his bread to someone who was hungrier than he; a father shielding his child; a mother trying to hold back her tears so her children would not see her pain—that was courage."[212]

And Wiesel then posed the questions. "Is there hope? Is there hope in memory?" "There must be. Without hope memory would be morbid and sterile. Without memory, hope would be empty of meaning, and above all empty of gratitude."[213]

King posited that a fifth characteristic of nonviolent resistance is that *it avoids not only external physical violence but also internal violence of the spirit*. The nonviolent resister not only refuses to shoot his opponent, but he also refuses to hate him. At the center of nonviolence stands the principle of agapic love. King elaborated on love as the center of nonviolence:

The nonviolent resister would contend that in the struggle for human dignity, the oppressed people of the world must not succumb to the temptation of becoming bitter or indulging in hate campaigns. To retaliate in kind would do nothing but intensify the existence of hatred in the universe. Along the way of life, someone must have sense enough and morality enough to cut off the chain of hate. This can only be done by projecting the ethic of love to the center of our lives.

King continued:

In speaking of love at this point, we are not referring to some sentimental and affectionate emotion. It would be nonsense to urge persons to love oppressors in an affectionate sense. Love in this context means understanding, redemptive goodwill. Here the Greek language comes to our aid. There are three words for love in the Greek New Testament. First, there is *eros*. In platonic philosophy *eros* meant the yearning of the souls for the realm of the divine. It has come now to mean a sort of aesthetic or romantic love. Second is *philia*, which means intimate affection between personal friends. *Philia* denotes a sort of reciprocal love; the person loves because he is loved. When we speak of loving those who oppose us, we refer to neither *eros* nor *philia*; we speak of a love that is expressed in the Greek word *agape*. *Agape* means understanding, redeeming goodwill for all men. It is an overflowing love, which is purely spontaneous, unmotivated, groundless, and creative. It is not set in motion by any quality or function of its object. It is the love of God operating in the human heart.

*Agape* is disinterested love. It is a love in which the individual seeks not his own good, but the good of his neighbor (1 Cor. 10:24). *Agape* does not begin by discriminating between worthy and unworthy people, or any quality people possess. It begins by loving others for their sakes. It is an entirely "neighbor-regarding concern for others," which discovers the neighbor in every man it meets. Therefore *agape* makes no distinction between friend and enemy; it is directed toward both. If one loves an individual merely on account of his friendliness, he loves him for the sake of the benefits to be gained from the friendship, rather than for the friend's own sake. Consequently, the best way to assure oneself that love is disinterested is to have love for the enemy-neighbor from whom you can expect no good in return, but only hostility and persecution.

Another basic point about *agape* is that it springs from the need of the other person – his need for belonging to the best in the human family. The Samaritan who helped the Jew on the Jericho Road was "good" because he responded to the human need that he was presented with. God's love is eternal and fails not because man needs his love. St. Paul assures us that the loving act of redemption was done "while we were yet sinners" - that is, at the point of our greatest need for love. Since the white man's personality is generally distorted by segregation, and his soul is greatly scarred, he needs the love of the Negro. The Negro must love the white man, because the white man needs his love to remove his tensions, insecurities and fears.

A sixth characteristic of nonviolent resistance for King, is that *it is based on the conviction that the universe is on the side of justice.* With regard to this, he said:

Consequently, the believer in nonviolence has deep faith in the future. This faith is another reason why the nonviolent resister can accept suffering without retaliation. For he knows that in his struggle for justice, he has cosmic companionship. It is true that there are devout believers in nonviolence who find it difficult to believe in a personal God. But even those persons believe in the existence of some creative force that works for universal wholeness. Whether we call it an unconscious process, an impersonal Brahman, or a Personal Being of matchless power and infinite love, there is a creative force in this universe that works to bring the disconnected aspects of reality into a harmonious whole.

## Conclusion

In the final analysis, nonviolent resistance hinges on the conviction that amidst injustice, evil, oppression, suffering and dehumanization, the arc of the moral universe is wide, and it always bends towards justice. Furthermore, this justice is ultimately expressed in the form of peaceful and *Beloved Community*.

What Martin Luther King, Jr. advocated for when he spoke of the Christian love-ethic was the *Beloved Community*. The *Beloved Community* is not something that is passive, weak and anemic but a loving community that is active, vibrant, transformational, and in many ways can be revolutionary and counter cultural, tough love.

On December 10, 1964, King became the youngest person to receive the Nobel Peace Prize at the age of 35. In his acceptance address in Oslo, Norway, King reiterated his commitment to the philosophy of nonviolence: "Nonviolence is the answer to the crucial political and moral questions of our time: the need for man to overcome oppression and violence without resorting to oppression and violence. Man must evolve for all human conflict a method which rejects revenge, aggression and retaliation. The foundation of such a method is love."[214]

# CHAPTER SEVEN

# OUT OF THE MOUNTAIN OF DESPAIR – MARTIN LUTHER KING, JR. AND HOPE

In one of his later sermons, "The Meaning of Hope," Martin Luther King, Jr. defined hope as that quality which is "necessary for life."[215] He asserted that hope was to be viewed as "animated and undergirded by faith and love." In his mind, if you had hope, you had faith in something. Thus, hope shares the belief that "all reality hinges on moral foundations."[216] For King, hope was the refusal to give up "despite overwhelming odds." This hope beckons us to love everybody – both our enemies and allies. It helps us to see that we can resist giving up on one another because our lives together are animated by the belief that God is present in each and every one of us, and in every circumstance.

## King, Hope and the American Dream

Today, many people would agree that a great deal of progress has been made in light of King's dream of equality and his call to action over the course of his 14-year public ministry. With the passage of the Civil Rights Act and Voting Rights Act in 1964 and 1965 respectively, greater opportunities for many women and persons of color in our society, the election in 2008 of Barack Hussein Obama as the first American president of African descent, and expanding engagement of persons across cultures and classes, we have seen concrete evidence of the realization of King's dream which was most clearly and demonstratively expressed during his August 1963 "I Have a Dream" speech at the March on Washington.

These are days of tremendous change and challenge. From the collapse of economies that affect most people – to wars that are now being fought around the world – to the proliferation of violence that affects many communities - to the healthcare crisis that results in millions of Americans still living without affordable, adequate healthcare – to the ever-expanding prison industrial complex, mass incarceration, and over-incarceration of Black and Brown people, where we are reminded by Michelle Alexander in her book, *The New Jim Crow* that we have more Black and Brown men in prison than we do in college - indeed, these are days of unprecedented change and challenge.

Perhaps, the most glaring signs of social distress in America today can be found in the lingering problem of racism. It is clear that race continues to matter in America, and that we are not yet at the place of being post-racial or post-racist in the churches or society. Michael Eric Dyson addresses this matter in his book, *Can You Hear Me Now?*, where he insists that the critical question that is before society today is not if we are yet a *post-racial* society, and the question is not even if we should strive to become post-racial, but the critical question is how might we move closer towards becoming a *post-racist* society?

Indeed, there are considerable challenges to arriving at a hope that is yet to be fully realized. In 1992, philosopher Cornel West authored an important book entitled, *Race Matters.* The book was written against the backdrop of the Los Angeles riots of April 1992, which followed the acquittal of the police officers charged in the beating of Rodney King, and the ensuing racial tensions in that city. In the book, West pointed to what he referred to as the "nihilism of Black America" – where a certain nothingness, meaninglessness, lovelessness and hopelessness seemed to have pervaded and permeated much of our society – particularly in urban contexts, and as it pertains to Black and Brown people. According to him at that time, race mattered in America, and thus we as a society must continue to attend to matters of race.

In light of these realities, realizing hope is not easy. In his 2008 book, *Hope on a Tightrope*, West laid the groundwork for a discourse on hope in its contemporary context. He cautioned against a false sense of security in hope, yet unborn. He posited that real hope is grounded in a particularly messy struggle and it can be betrayed by naive projections of a better future that ignore the necessity of doing real work. For West, real hope is closely connected to attributes like courage, faith, freedom and wisdom. It comes out of a history of struggle, and points to a future filled with the possibilities of promise and progress.[217]

One of the things that Martin Luther King, Jr. intimated in his 1963 "I Have a Dream" speech was a hope that God would "hew out of the mountain of despair, a stone of hope." The despair that he alluded to then was capsulated in what he deemed to be the "triplets of evil" – racism, poverty (classism) and war (militarism). In King's estimation, these were the major categories of the social disease that afflicted America then, and thus there was the need for the struggle for civil rights, human rights and equal rights, and thus also a need for the March on Washington, the Poor People's Campaign, opposition to the War in Vietnam, and a renewed call/commitment to prophetic action.

As King spoke at the Lincoln Memorial on that sunlit day in August 1963, he shared with the crowd, the nation and the world a compelling dream – a vision of the *Beloved Community* - of a world where every "child would be judged not by the color of their skin, but by the content of their character." He articulated a hope that America would live up to the true meaning of its creed as found in the Declaration of Independence, "We hold these truths to be self-evident, that all (people) are created equal."

A part of the moral prerogative of churches, civil and human rights organizations, and all other institutions and persons concerned about the common good and well-being of our world today remains that of speaking truthfully and hopefully to the critical moral and social issues of the contemporary age, and then working to bring about progressive change. The task ahead is to help devise and articulate a framework for engaging in critical and constructive advocacy for the disinherited among us – the poor, violated, suffering and oppressed.

And an important aspect of the churches' prophetic task is also to be self-critical as it pertains to issues such as the proliferation of the prosperity gospel, the lack of activism in many circles, the inability or unwillingness of the churches today to speak and act prophetically on matters of contemporary concern such as war, domestic terror and gun violence, the widening gap between the rich and the poor in America and around the world, the ongoing proliferation of racial (and other forms of) bigotry, the marginalization of too many in our society, along with the generally violent and misogynistic nature of hip hop and other expressions of popular culture.

### Barack Obama and Hope Renewed

At the historic election of Barack H. Obama as the 44th President of the United States on November 11, 2008, many people seemed to sense (and hope) that his election had ushered in an age of post-racism and post-racialism in America – and perhaps around the world.

In his 2006 book, *The Audacity of Hope*, then-Senator Barack Obama offered words of caution to America in thinking that we may have arrived at becoming "post-racial" or that we already live in a color-blind society, and that we are beyond the need for discourse and critical engagement as it regards race, racism and related forms of oppression and injustice. He wrote:

> To say that we are one people is not to suggest that race no longer matters – that the fight for equality has been won, or that the problems that minorities face in

this country today are largely self-inflicted. We know the statistics: On almost every single socioeconomic indicator, from infant mortality to life expectancy to employment to home ownership, black and Latino Americans in particular lag far behind their white counterparts.[218]

In a major address prior to his election entitled "A More Perfect Union", delivered on March 18, 2008 during his presidential campaign, Obama offered an analysis of the prevalence of racial tensions which have continued to define the relationship between the black and white communities in America. Obama asserted that to simply shelve anger or "wish away" the race problem in America could prove to be seriously detrimental. Unambiguously, he pointed to a belief that race factors into the opportunities provided to each American citizen.

To support his assertion, he noted that inferior school systems today are often the ones that were segregated fifty years ago. He further asserted that the history of racism in America is undeniably at the root of the lack of opportunities for African Americans today. In light of this, it is necessary for all Americans to unite and battle racial prejudices and oppression. According to Obama, in order to move to a "more perfect union", people of all races need to recognize the historically oppressive and tyrannical nature of racism and its impact on the black experience in America.

A good deal of the political discourse during the 2008 presidential primaries focused on then-Senator Barack Obama's membership at Trinity United Church of Christ in

Chicago, and his 20-year relationship with Rev. Dr. Jeremiah Wright, the church's pastor at that time. On the surface, many of the concerns levied against Obama in light of his relationship with Wright centered on comments that Wright had made in several sermons in which he offered pointed, and what some considered to have been derogatory critiques of America and the Bush presidential administration in the aftermath of the 2001 terrorist attacks and in light of the then war in Iraq.

In light of Wright's role as a prophetic leader in the church, community and across the nation for over thirty years, perhaps then it is not coincidental that like him, who in 2007 expressed his opposition to the war in Iraq, Martin Luther King, Jr., (40 years prior) on April 4, 1967 at Riverside Church in New York City – in a sermon entitled, "Beyond Vietnam – A Time to Break Silence" – similarly expressed in vehement terms his opposition to the war in Vietnam.[219] King stated:

> At this point I should make it clear that while I have tried in these last few minutes to give a voice to the voiceless on Vietnam and to understand the arguments of those who are called enemy, I am as deeply concerned about our troops there as anything else. For it occurs to me that what we are submitting them to in Vietnam is not simply the brutalizing process that goes on in any war where armies face each other and seek to destroy. We are adding cynicism to the process of death, for they must know

after a short period there that none of the things we claim to be fighting for are really involved.

King further expressed his concerns about the Vietnam war.[220] He said:

Somehow this madness must cease. We must stop now. I speak as a child of God and brother of the suffering poor of Vietnam. I speak for those whose land is being laid waste, whose homes are being destroyed, whose culture is being subverted. I speak for the poor of America who are paying the double price of smashed hopes at home and death corruption in Vietnam.

In a speech at the University of Michigan in 1962, King shared a point that he would make on several other occasions. He pointed out that we are faced with a choice in our life together, and that we will either learn to live together as (sisters and brothers), or perish together as fools.[221]

### *Finding Hope amidst Despair*

In many ways, America is a contradiction laying in the metaphysical conundrum of hope and despair – with wealth and poverty, abundance and scarcity being simultaneously extant. In the wealthiest nation in the world, with abundance across many sectors, income and wealth disparity among the richest and the rest of Americans is most evident in the plight of the poorest Americans – those who are housing and food insecure, with related forms of scarcity in adequate healthcare, nutrition, clean water, education, employment, safety, technology and transportation. Mohandas Gandhi intimated years ago that "poverty is the worst form of violence."

Howard Thurman, in "Through the Coming Year" offered a confessional prayer that captures the nature of the existential despair that we all may struggle with in seeking to do God's will –

In my confusion I shall often say
the word that is not true
and do the thing of which I am ashamed.
There will be errors in the mind
and great inaccuracies of judgment.

In seeking the light,
I shall again and again find myself
walking in the darkness.[222]

Today, I propose that we live within the crucible of *Ten Contemporary Social Plagues*: (1) Poverty, income/wealth inequality and inequity; (2) Racism and xenophobia ; (3) Misogyny and violence against women, and lack of comparable worth; (4) Lack of full attention to the environment, global warming and climate change; (5) Under-education and miseducation of large segments of society; (6) Financial profiteering of the gun lobby, and gun violence; (7) The growing prison industrial complex, financial profiteering on incarceration, and the over-incarceration of Black and Brown people; (8) Anti-immigration and immigrant bashing; (9) Police brutality; and (10) Militarism and terrorism (domestic and foreign).[223]

These ten contemporary social plagues tend to make hope fleeting. Yet, amidst despair, hope beckons the churches and society to proactively and prophetically act to address the plight of those who have the least among us – many Black and Brown persons, our homeless and hungry neighbors, and those of our siblings who are immigrants - and to see poverty as in and of itself, inflicting violence upon its victims – violence which stains the soul and dignity of persons, violence which affects persons' physical well-being and threatens their lives, and violence which impacts the potential and possibility of individuals and society as a whole.

Some of what underlies our will to such violence on the soul, and our inability and/or unwillingness to address it is rooted, again, in the very real and deep racial and class divides that exist among us. Ta-Nehisi Coates in his book, *Between the World and Me*, writes about growing up on the streets of Baltimore, and states that "race is the child of racism, not the father."[224] By extension it could be argued that class is the child of classism, not the mother. The concomitant evils of racism and classism serve as severe detriments to bringing about wholeness for those among us who find ourselves living on the margins of society, and these evils are ultimately detrimental to the realization of the *Beloved Community.*

Our divine and moral imperative, amidst such existential despair, is to speak out and act out – individually and collectively – with and for our neighbors - to speak out and act out with compassion and justice. Our divine and moral imperative is to speak out and act out in ways that address the immediate needs of God's people who must endure existential despair by providing adequate shelter, food, clean water, clothing, healthcare and safety – while also addressing the serious systemic political, economic and moral concerns that lead us to ask why our sisters and brothers are forced to endure such existential despair in the first place.

With all that continues to plague America and the world, there's the need to renew our commitment to Martin Luther King, Jr.'s dream, and to heed a call to action. Where might hope reside in and among us as we look to the future? King stated that "The hopeless individual is the dead individual." In his view hope had a transformative quality that keeps human beings "alive" both spiritually and psychologically.[225] Hope, therefore, is "one of the basic structures of an adequate life."

In the third century, Augustine, the Bishop of Hippo is attributed with intimating that "Hope has two beautiful daughters; their names are *Anger* and *Courage. Anger at the way things are, and Courage to see that they do not remain the way they are."* Hope does not settle for the status quo – whatever it is – but always pushes towards a better future.

In *Theology of Hope,* Jürgen Moltmann intimated that:
> "Hope alone is to be called 'realistic', because it alone takes seriously the possibilities with which all reality is fraught. It does not take things as they

167

happen to stand or to lie, but as progressing, moving things with possibilities of change. Only as long as the world and the people in it are in a fragmented and experimental state which is not yet resolved, is there any sense in earthly hopes."[226]

Moltmann posits an eschatologically-centered perspective on hope that focuses on the hope that Christ's Resurrection brings. For him, the hope of the Christian faith is hope in the resurrection of Christ crucified. Accordingly, through faith we are bound to Christ, and as such we have the hope of the resurrected Christ, and can anticipate his return. Hope and faith, Moltmann posits, depend on each other to remain true and substantial; and only with both may one find "not only a consolation in suffering, but also the protest of the divine promise against suffering.[227]

Hope strengthens faith, helps believers live lives of love, and directs persons toward a new creation of all things. It creates in us a "passion for the possible." As Moltmann asserts, "For our knowledge and comprehension of reality, and our reflections on it, that means at least this: that in the medium of hope our theological concepts become not judgments which nail reality down to what it is, but anticipations which show reality its prospects and its future possibilities."[228]

King framed his vision of hope within the context of the *Beloved Community*. Hope can be found in the possibilities that we will continue to discover ways to capitalize on those experiences and encounters that will lead to us being intentional, authentic and radically inclusive community. Hope for a better future is rooted and grounded in our shared potential and commitment to change the world for the better. The church and society today look quite different from the church and society of fifty years ago. Progress can be seen in many areas. And yet there is still much work that lies ahead of us. This is the hope that must be realized if the church is to be the church, the *Beloved Community*, that King imagined, and which Christ calls it to become.

## *Is There No Balm?*

The prophet Jeremiah offered a vision of hope for a people experiencing despair and exile in a strange land. In the sixth century B.C.E., the Israelites were in Babylon – alienated from their land, from their God, and – many of them - from their loved ones.

We can imagine that the Israelites experienced what Friedrich Nietzsche, Cornel West and other philosophers have come to refer to as an apparent nihilism – an apparent nothingness, meaninglessness, lovelessness and hopelessness that can come to define the existence of a people amidst such despair. In Psalm 137, while in Babylonian exile, the Israelites expressed their anguish:

> *By the rivers of Babylon we sat and wept*
> *when we remembered Zion.*
> *There on the poplars*

*we hung our harps,*
*for there our captors asked us for songs,*
*our tormentors demanded songs of joy;*
*they said, "Sing us one of the songs of Zion!"*
*How can we sing the songs of the Lord*
*while in a foreign land? (Psalm 137:1-4)*

It is against this backdrop of the apparent existential nihilism of the Israelites in Babylon that Jeremiah shares these words of hope:

*"For surely, I know the plans I have for you, says the Lord, plans for your welfare (shalom, wholeness, well-being), and not for your harm, plans to give you a future with hope." (Jeremiah 29:11)*

On numerous occasions, Martin Luther King, Jr. pointed out that the nature of hope is evident in questions posed by the prophet Jeremiah –

*"Is there no balm in Gilead; is there no physician there? Why then has the health of my poor people not been restored?"* (Jeremiah 8:22)

King intimated that amidst the oppression that many black people had experienced in America – through slavery, Jim Crow and persistent racism - people of faith in God were able to convert the *question marks* of the prophet Jeremiah's lament, into *exclamation points* as they affirmed their faith and hope in the living and life-giving God, in a song. And so they sang in affirmation of their faith, with blessed assurance:

*There is a balm in Gilead,*
*to make the wounded whole*
*There is a balm in Gilead,*
*To heal the sin-sick soul.*
*Sometimes I feel discouraged,*
*And think my work's in vain*
*And then the Holy Spirit*
*Revives my soul again!* [229]

King's ultimate hope rested in the prospects that the "World House" – *the Beloved Community* – would someday be realized. He stated in *Where Do We Go from Here?* that, "Our hope for creative living in this "World House" that we have inherited lies in our ability to reestablish the moral ends of our lives in personal character and social justice. Without this spiritual and moral reawakening we shall destroy ourselves in the misuse of our own instruments."[230]

In the final analysis, the realization of the *Beloved Community*, for King, depends on never giving up hoping amidst despair Indeed, today, he might affirm the encouraging sentiments of the great poet Langston Hughes to:

*Hold fast to dreams,*
*For when dreams die,*
*Life is a broken winged bird*
*That cannot fly.*

*Hold fast to dreams,*
*For when dreams go,*
*Life is a barren field*
*Frozen with snow.*

## CHAPTER EIGHT

## I'VE SEEN THE PROMISED LAND - MARTIN LUTHER KING, JR. AND THE 21st CENTURY QUEST FOR THE BELOVED COMMUNITY

Beyond his accomplishments in the Civil Rights movement, and even beyond his constant articulation and yearning for the church and society to realize what it means to be the *Beloved Community,* Martin Luther King, Jr.'s signature contribution to the human project was a reminder that whoever we are, whatever our skin color, whoever our parents are, from wherever we have come, we are "somebody" in God's sight.

Robert F. Kennedy, captured the essence of King's vision in Kennedy's remarks on the evening of King's assassination on April 4, 1968. "What we need in the United States is not division; what we need in the United States is not hatred; what we need in the United States is not violence and lawlessness, but is love, and wisdom and compassion toward one another, and a feeling of justice toward those who still suffer within our country, whether they be white or whether they be black."[231]

## *"Tell them about the Dream, Martin!"*

On August 28, 1963, King gave a 17-minute speech before an estimated 250,000 people on the steps of the Lincoln Memorial in Washington, DC, as the culminating remarks for the national March on Washington for Jobs and Freedom. Much of the world is now familiar with the vision of America that King proceeded to share with the world that day in what has come to be known as his "I Have a Dream" speech.

King's prepared written remarks lasted about eleven minutes, and he had almost finished when renown gospel singer Mahalia Jackson encouraged him to, *"Tell them about the dream, Martin!"* Jackson sparked an extemporaneous, improvisational expression in King where he then proceeded for the next six minutes to share a poetic refrain he had preached before. In that concluding recitation, King essentially described to the world his dream of the *Beloved Community,* when girls and boys of all races could play together and go to school together, and where people would be judged by the content of their character, and not the color of their skin.

What is often lost amidst his eloquent words in the "I Have a Dream" speech is that earlier in the recitation, King spoke of something equally as important to those who heard it then, and us to who read it today. He spoke of *"the fierce urgency of now,"* the need for immediate, "vigorous and positive action" in overcoming racism and other "isms" in society.

In his sketch of the *"fierce urgency of now"*, King reiterated sentiments that he had shared on several other occasions. He said, *"We are now faced with the fact that tomorrow is today. We are confronted with the fierce urgency of now. In this unfolding conundrum of life and history, there "is" such a thing as being too late. This is no time for apathy or complacency. This is a time for vigorous and positive action."*

In an earlier speech in 1963 in Detroit, Michigan, King had similarly alluded to this fierce urgency. He said, *"But these events that are taking place in our nation tell us something else. They tell us that the Negro and his allies in the white community now recognize the urgency of the moment... And so this social revolution taking place can be summarized in three little words. They are not big words. One does not need an extensive vocabulary to understand them. They are the words "all," "here," and "now." We want all of our rights, we want them here, and we want them now."*

### The Letter from Birmingham Jail and the Cultural Captivity of the Church

In April 1963, while imprisoned in the Birmingham (Alabama) City Jail, King wrote a letter that was first published in *The Christian Century*. It became a classic appeal for rights denied blacks for 344 years. His Birmingham Jail letter, commonly referred to as The Letter from Birmingham Jail, was specifically written to address eight white Birmingham clergymen and their congregations who in 1963 were insisting on gradual, moderate approaches to changing the atrocious racial and social injustices occurring in Birmingham and across the state of Alabama, and the nation at that time.

Highlighting the significance of what transpired in Birmingham in the spring of 1963, Taylor Branch asserts that there was no historical precedent for Birmingham in April and May of 1963, when the power balance of a great nation turned not on clashing armies or global commerce but on the youngest student demonstrators of African descent, down to first- and second-graders.[232]  Only the literature of the Passover ascribes such impact to the fate of minors, and never before was a country transformed, arguably redeemed, by the active moral witness of schoolchildren.[233]

For King, the Christian churches were ideally to be fertile ground for the enactment of the *Beloved Community*. But in his assessment, churches had been found wanting in the sphere of prophetic witness, and had too often remained complicit in their silence and complacent in their inaction. In his Birmingham Jail letter, he stated that, "There comes a time when silence becomes betrayal."  In his analysis, the churches had too often been found in the position of being the captive instrument of society and culture.

In his response to the eight Birmingham clergymen, King described the cultural captivity of the church:

> I have heard numerous religious leaders of the South call upon their worshippers to comply with a desegregation decision because it is the law, but I have longed to hear white ministers say, "Follow this

decree because integration is morally right and the Negro is your brother." In the midst of blatant injustices inflicted upon the Negro, I have watched white churches stand on the sideline and merely mouth pious irrelevancies and sanctimonious trivialities. In the midst of a mighty struggle to rid our nation of racial and economic injustice, I have heard so many ministers say, "those are social issues with which the Gospel has no real concern", and I have watched so many churches commit themselves to a completely other-worldly religion which made a strange distinction between body and soul, the sacred and the secular.[234]

Dietrich Bonhoeffer addressed similar cultural captivity of the church when he intimated to the German churches in the 1930s and 40s amidst the injustices and atrocities of Nazi Germany against Jewish, gay, "non-white" people and others that "silence in the face of evil is itself evil. God will not hold us guiltless. Not to speak is to speak, and not to act is to act."[235]

In his Birmingham Jail letter, King also argued for acting against unjust laws. He stated, "There are *just* laws and there are *unjust* laws." With St. Augustine, King reasoned that a truly unjust law was no law at all. As he argued his case, King called attention to the burgeoning and potentially violent Black Muslim movement, which loomed as a threat should white Americans continue to deny rights. He asserted, "It is made up of people who have lost faith in America, who have absolutely repudiated Christianity, and who have concluded that the white man is an incurable 'devil'". The Negro church offered the best hope for nonviolent change.[236]

In distinguishing between a just and an unjust law, King intimated that "Any law that uplifts human personality is just. Any law that degrades human personality is unjust."[237] He based his understanding of just and unjust laws largely on the teachings of Thomas Aquinas on natural law in *Summa Theologica*. King further intimated that "One has not only a legal, but a moral responsibility to obey just laws. Conversely, one has a moral responsibility to disobey unjust laws".[238] This is the nature of civil (and holy) disobedience.

Then, a few months after his Birmingham letter, at the March on Washington, DC on August 28, 1963, King again addressed the matters of gradualism and moderation, and argued again for acting against unjust laws in seeking to move with fierce urgency toward racial, social and economic justice for all people.

### King and the Dimensions of Social Disembodiment Today

Over the course of American history, as has been intimated herein, racism has been America's original sin, and today, racism continues to be *the elephant in America's living room*. Social disembodiment can be defined and characterized as any structures, processes, beliefs, ideologies or behaviors that serve to separate and segregate one or more humans, and serve to create communal disunity, disintegration and disengagement. Racism, sexism and classism are some of the most pronounced forms and manifestations of social disembodiment today. In America, in the churches and society, racism continues to be a primary way that social disembodiment is manifest and experienced, and there exist intersections with sexism, classism and other forms of social disembodiment.

It is important that social disembodiment, and particularly race division today, be viewed against the historical backdrop of racism in American society. In 1903, African-American sociologist W. E. B. DuBois asserted that "the problem of the 20th century is the problem of the color-line" (*The Souls of Black Folk*). In 1944, Swedish sociologist Gunnar Myrdal discussed the plight of African Americans (the Negro Problem) within the context of what he referred to as the "American dilemma" (*An American Dilemma: The Negro Problem and Modern Democracy*). And in 1968, the Kerner Commission Report, based on a study which President Lyndon B. Johnson had requested in light of the civil unrest and riots that had broken out in several cities across the United States, summarized the state of race relations in America by noting that "America is a nation of two societies, one black and one white, separate and unequal." This divide continues to exist some 50 years later.

During a visit to the Southern Poverty Law Center in Montgomery, Alabama in April 2019, I and others who were a part of the delegation were informed that there are over 950 hate-related groups currently identified in the U.S., up from about 800 in 2008, and that this number has continued to rise since the 2016 U.S. presidential election. This rise in hate-related groups in America (and the incumbent violence related to them) is to be viewed against the historic backdrop of over 4075 lynchings of Black Americans in 12 Southern states from 1877-1950, as documented by the Equal Justice Initiative, also in Montgomery. According to the Southern Poverty Law Center, the number of neo-Nazi groups in the U.S. has increased by 22 percent since the 2017 U.S. presidential inauguration.

A part of America's sense of who it says it is is etched in one of our national credos – the Latin phrase *e-pluribus unum* – "Out of Many One." The implication here is that in the U.S, we have been, and continue to be a nation of "many". We are many cultures and ethnicities (we are largely a nation of immigrants and refugees), many classes and social locations, religions, geographies, female and male, with many perspectives, persuasions and ways of identifying what it means to be human. And yet, the vision that we say we share within the context of this "many" is of somehow also becoming "one".

In any event, today we experience the challenge of living into the grand vision of what it means to become *e-pluribus unum*. And so, perhaps it is "divides" in the churches and society which most clearly characterize the social disembodiment we experience today. These "divides" are seen in that we are Indigenous, Hispanic, Asian, White and Black, LGBTQI+ and "straight", poor, working class, middle class and wealthy, Republican, Democrat and Independent, southern and northern, western and eastern, midwestern and southwestern, rural, suburban and urban, conservative, moderate and liberal, evangelical, centrist and progressive, non-denominational and mainline, Protestant and Catholic, Muslim, Jewish, Hindu, Buddhist, Sikh, and many other persuasions. These "divides" are also seen in that – politically and religiously - we are red, blue and purple (indeed, various shades of purple).

In light of King's ideal of the *Beloved Community*, and in light of the church's striving to be the body of Christ (the embodiment of Christ), questions then remain. How do these various forms of division, difference, disintegration, and disengagement effectively serve to perpetuate social disembodiment in the churches and society today? And how might they be addressed?

In her book, *Stand Your Ground: Black Bodies and the Justice of God,* Kelly Brown Douglas posits that such disembodiment can be seen through the crucifixion of Jesus on the Cross, and the death of Trayvon Martin in Florida in 2012. "Both Jesus and Trayvon were members of despised minorities. Both were feared because of who they were... Both were accused of sedition. Both were killed by the "rule of law."[239]

This matter of disembodiment can also be seen in pronounced ways in the rhetorical and existential attacks on black women's bodies in some of the highest places of our society today – in politics, entertainment, sports and even the church. Cheryl Townsend Gilkes intimates in her essay, "The Loves and Troubles of African American Women's Bodies" that:

All human experience is embodied experience and the consequences of cultural humiliation are most dramatically shown with reference to the body. Not only is experience embodied, but stereotypes, pernicious cultural representations of people, are also embodied images.[240]

Why is this important for the churches and society today? Steven Vertovec, in his essay, "Super-diversity and its Implications", places the phenomenon of social change in the context of what he terms 'super-diversity'. Vertovec asserts that today Britain can be characterized by 'super-diversity,' which is a construct that he argues is intended to underline a level and kind of societal complexity surpassing anything that Britain has previously experienced. Where in the past Britain's immigrant and ethnic minority population has conventionally been characterized by large, well-organized African-Caribbean and South Asian communities of citizens originally from Commonwealth countries or formerly colonial territories, the country's diversity is now characterized by persons from a broader spectrum of geographic, religious and ethnic backgrounds.[241]

Although Vertovec focuses primarily on the changing dynamics of diversity in Britain, these changes, in many respects, mirror those occurring in the United States. Vertovec's thesis of 'super-diversity' holds in that in the United States over the past several decades, research data shows that the U.S. continues to become more diverse, 'different' and 'super-diverse'. In the U.S., super-diversity is seen in that –

- The non-Hispanic white population in the U.S. is expected to fall below 50% by 2042, but non-Hispanic Whites will remain the largest single ethnic group.[242]
- Non-Hispanic Whites are the slowest growing segment of the U.S. population at .5%.[243]
- There are at least 56 million Hispanics in the U.S. (16% of the population). Hispanic and Latino populations are projected to make up 30% of the U.S. population by 2050.[244]
- Asians make up 5.8% of the U.S. population, and this percentage is projected to rise to at least 7.8% by 2050. Asians make up 36% of immigrants, exceeding the percentage of Hispanics and Latinos. China is the fastest growing immigrant group in the U.S., passing Mexico.[245]
- The percentage of Blacks is projected to remain steady at 13% through 2050.
- By 2040, Islam will surpass Judaism to become the second largest religion in the U.S. due to higher immigration and birth rates.[246]
- There are at least 3.3 million Muslims in the U.S., and that number is likely to double by 2050.[247]

***Perspectives on the Excluding Church***

Growing super-diversity in America can also be seen in the fact that according to U.S. Census Bureau data, in 1960 non-Hispanic whites comprised over 88 percent of the U.S. population, and in 2010, non-Hispanic whites totaled about 61 percent of the U.S. population. These social indicators, factors and trends effectively correlate with the problem of the excluding church. In their book, *Divided by Faith: Evangelical Religion and the Problem of Race,* Michael Emerson and Christian Smith developed a theory to explain why churches are racially exclusive, hyper-segregated enclaves despite Christianity's ideals about being inclusive. According to Emerson and Smith, Americans choose where and with whom to worship; race is one of the most important grounds on which they choose; so the more choices they have, the more their religious institutions will be segregated.[248]

Through sociological analysis, Emerson and Smith tested their theory and found it to be valid. Churches are more segregated than schools, workplaces or neighborhoods. The least segregated sector of American society is also the least governed by choice; it's the military. Because white Protestants are the largest religious community in the U.S., they have the greatest choice as to with whom to gather. The authors point out that ninety-five percent of churches are effectively racially segregated, with at least 80 percent or more of their members being of the same race.[249]

The result of hyper-segregation in religious bodies, along racial and class lines is that about 5 percent of religious congregations in the U.S. can be fairly considered to be multicultural/multiracial, with the majority of Christians engaging in what sociologists call homophily, or the desire to congregate with "birds of the same feather," with their congregations reflecting ethnoracial particularism.[250]

Martin Luther King, Jr. saw that the problem of an excluding church and the type of hyper-segregation that has been depicted is rooted in the fact that too many Christians have not clearly understood or faithfully followed the central personality of the faith, Jesus Christ.

In his seminal 1949 work *Jesus and the Disinherited*, Howard Thurman wrote regarding the excluding church:

> To those who need profound succor and strength to enable them to live in the present with dignity and creativity, Christianity often has been sterile and of little avail. The conventional Christian word is muffled, confused and vague. Too often the price exacted by society for security and respectability is that the Christian movement in its formal expression must be on the side of the strong against the weak. This is a matter of tremendous significance, for it reveals to what extent a religion that was born of people acquainted with persecution and suffering has become the cornerstone of a civilization and of nations whose very position in modern life has too often been secured by ruthless use of power applied to weak and defenseless people.[251]

In reflecting on the state of the church in his day, Thurman further wrote in 1954:

> It is in order now at last to raise the question: Is the witness of the church in our society the unfolding of such an idea as we see manifested in the religious experience and the life of Jesus? Whatever may be the delimiting character of the historical development

of the church, the simple fact remains that at the present moment in our society, as an institution, the church is divisive and discriminating, even within its fellowship. It is divided into dozens of splinters. This would indicate that it is essentially sectarian in character. As an institution there is no such thing as the church. There has to be some kind of church..."[252]

King insisted that racism is one of the key barriers to authentic community. In a September 1967 speech entitled "The Challenge to Social Scientists", delivered to the American Psychological Association, King stated:

White America is seeking to keep the walls of segregation substantially intact while the evolution of society and the Negro's desperation is causing them to crumble. The white majority, unprepared and unwilling to accept radical structural change, is resisting and producing chaos while complaining that if there were no chaos, orderly change would come." [253]

For King, community is essential to life, meaning and wholeness. It is out of this deep sense of burden and passion for community that he was able to see how detrimental and destructive racism and other forms of social division are to community because they deny, denigrate and destroy people (personality) based on external and surface qualities. This is the essence of social disembodiment, and is clearly evident in the excluding church.

### *Charlottesville and American Racism Today*

The events that transpired in Charlottesville, Virginia during the second weekend of August 2017 are perhaps the clearest emblem of social embodiment in America today. These events were not surprising to many people familiar with the history, and acquainted with the legacy of race and racism in America. As young white men wielded torches through a college town, the home of the University of Virginia - the school founded by one of America's founding fathers, Thomas Jefferson - and chanted anti-Semitic and racist slogans, the truth that was revealed over the course of that weekend is that the so-called alt-right, white supremacy, white nationalism and neo-Nazism is alive in America.

Having traveled Virginia Highway 29 all of my life from Washington, D.C. to Lynchburg, Virginia to visit my extended family, I've passed through Charlottesville, and ridden past the University of Virginia campus dozens of times. It has always been, and continues to be my experience and sense that in the rural communities surrounding Charlottesville and the University of Virginia, non-white people are not always welcome and racist elements have existed over the years, and do so today.

In the words of Malcolm X, "the chickens came home to roost" in Charlottesville in August 2017. What occurred there didn't happen coincidentally or by accident, but is the offspring of over a decade of a breeding politics of race, division, hate and fear in America that has become much more pronounced and vitriolic, and at points, violent in the last few years. Indeed, Charlottesville confirmed again that *'racism is the elephant in America's living room'*.

The very nature of racism is that it is rooted in hatred. There's no conceivable way in space and time (metaphysically) that love and hate can co-exist. The two cannot occupy the same space and time. Racism and white supremacy, in any of its forms, is rooted in hatred, and those who are racists do not and cannot love those whom they deem to be racially inferior.

What happened in Charlottesville was also a reminder that history is the parent of the present and future. Alabama and Virginia are the homes of Jefferson Davis and the Confederacy. If Alabama is the cradle of the Confederacy, then Virginia is its second seed-bed.

It is interesting then that things came to greater light as to the ongoing race problem in America in Charlottesville against the backdrop of not only the legacies of Confederate general Robert E. Lee and Confederate president Jefferson Davis, but against the backdrop of the oppressive and complex legacy of Thomas Jefferson, Montebello, Sally Hemings, and Jefferson's "Notes on the State of Virginia" (1785), in which, based on his Enlightenment Theory of race and sub-humanity, Jefferson questioned the requisite abilities of Black and Native American persons to reason.

Some who defended the events in Charlottesville, argued that the symbols which were the focal points of the weekend's events – confederate monuments and flags – have little, to no real meaning and connection to what is going on in contemporary America. But as Paul Tillich expounded upon in his *Systematic Theology II*, the very nature of symbols is that they invariably have meaning attached to them. The same symbol could mean different things to different people. Whatever one's perspective, in America, the hundreds of remaining Confederate monuments (some of which were the focal point of events in Charlottesville), the thousands of Confederate flags spread across America, the visible display of swastikas, people parading in public in white robes, images of torches, lynching trees, strange fruit, faces at bottoms of wells, and churches burning mean something to each of us within the context of the past, present and future of the nation.

A large part of the ongoing legacy of the display of Confederate monuments and other symbols across the land (in the South and North), and the pain attached to them for many Americans, has to be understood against the backdrop of the terrible atrocities - the concomitant suffering and death - of the American slave trade, which lasted for 246 years, and the ensuing years of politics of nullification and redemption, and Jim Crow. There's no historically valid way to detach the American slave trade from the rise of the Confederacy in the 19th century, the politics of redemption and nullification of the Black Reconstruction and Jim Crow through the 20th century, and Charlottesville today. For many people, these monuments and symbols point to the condoning, celebrating, and honoring of division and hatred, and minimizing and denying of the dehumanizing realities of slavery in America, the likes of which has not occurred at any other time or place in the civilized world.

What transpired in Charlottesville in 2017 also shed light on the fact that the faces of domestic terrorism and neo-Nazism in America today are in large measure young white males who have perpetrated mass murder - like Dylann Roof, Sean Urbanski and James Alex Fields, among others. And while some of America's national leadership has continued to work at revising and pushing immigration policies designed to keep entire classes of people out of the nation based on their religion and/or nationality (e.g. Muslims, Syrians, Mexicans and Central Americans), devising policies to build border walls, and revising policies allowing for the building of more privately owned prison facilities that will disproportionately house Black and Brown people, thus perpetuating what Michelle Alexander refers to as the "New Jim Crow" in America - the uncomfortable truth reiterated with the events in Charlottesville, and the shoes that continue to hurt America's feet as a nation is that racism remains an extant - living, breathing and breeding - reality around many dinner tables, in club houses, board rooms, government chambers, locker rooms, classrooms, and church pulpits and pews across America, and until this is faced and fixed, events like those which occurred in Charlottesville will continue to rear their ugly head.

The further truth that was revealed in Charlottesville is that as the so-called alt-right, white supremacy and neo-Nazism are alive, there will be no progress and overcoming this evil without struggle. Frederick Douglass intimated in the 19th century that there can be no progress without struggle, and that "power concedes nothing without a demand", and Fannie Lou Hamer in the 1950s and 60s similarly persistently asserted that progress comes through perseverance even when we are "sick and tired of being sick and tired."

A place of national lament is found in that it takes tragedies like Charlottesville for people of conscience to begin to raise our collective voices against evil and oppression. The concern is then that after the light has fully dimmed on events like Charlottesville, the nation then returns to business, silence and inaction as usual.

As it regards the American Christian churches' complicity with what happened in Charlottesville, and what's likely to happen elsewhere, Jim Wallis in his book *America's Original Sin*, posits that America remains at a point of soul searching and reckoning with its "original sin" - racism. He asserts that "Racism is rooted in sin – or evil, as nonreligious people might prefer – which goes deeper than politics, pointing fingers, partisan maneuvers, blaming and name calling. We can get to a better place only if we go to that morally deeper place.[254] Wallis further asserts, as it regards the Christian church and theology, that "White nationalism is not just racist, it's the anti-Christ."[255]

Michael Eric Dyson posits in his 2017 book, *Tears We Cannot Stop: A Sermon to White America*, that eventually the Christian churches of America (especially white churches) will have to have a Holy conversation about racism in the church and society. The truth of the matter is that a number of the members of the so-called alt-right, KKK, neo-Nazis, 'patriots' and white nationalists who went to Charlottesville in August 2017, raised unholy hell and inflicted unholy violence and death, and many of their sympathizers, worship in "Christian" churches on any given Sunday morning. Over the 241-year history of the nation, while there may have been subtle, episodic hints of such Holy conversation, to which Dyson alludes, as it regards race and racism, it has not happened in full substance anywhere, among any Christian denomination or non-denomination. Only when such Holy conversations, and then Holy engagement, occur in earnest will real racial redemption and reconciliation begin, and only then will Holy transformation occur.

In Montgomery, Alabama, there's a Civil Rights Memorial on the grounds of the Southern Poverty Law Center that displays the names of 40 persons of diverse backgrounds, across racial and class lines, who were martyred for the cause of racial and social justice in America. The names on the memorial are representative of thousands of others who have died, and include Emmett Till, Viola Liuzzo, Martin Luther King, Jr., James Reeb, Jimmy Lee Jackson, Addie Mae Collins, Cynthia Wesley, Carole Robertson, Carol Denise McNair, Medgar Evers, Andrew Goodman, James Chaney and Michael Schwerner. It is clear now that the name Heather Heyer, who was killed on that weekend in August 2017 in Charlottesville, became a part of that company of martyred witnesses who died for the cause of freedom and justice for all people.

### Where Do we Go from Here: Chaos or Community?

In 1967, Martin Luther King, Jr. published his final book entitled, *Where Do We Go from Here: Chaos or*

*Community?*. The book's publication was subsequent to a speech that King delivered with the same title at the 11th Annual Southern Christian Leadership Conference Convention in Atlanta, Georgia on August 16, 1967. In the speech, and subsequently in the book, King essentially offered his impression of the state of America and the world in terms of the movement towards the *Beloved Community*. King intimated his overarching concerns:

> I'm concerned about a better world. I'm concerned about justice; I'm concerned about brotherhood; I'm concerned about truth. And when one is concerned about that, he can never advocate violence. For through violence you may murder a murderer, but you can't murder murder. Through violence you may murder a liar, but you can't establish truth. Through violence you may murder a hater, but you can't murder hate through violence. Darkness cannot put out darkness; only light can do that.[256]

He continued:

> And I say to you, I have also decided to stick with love, for I know that love is ultimately the only answer to mankind's problems. And I'm going to talk about it everywhere I go. I know it isn't popular to talk about it in some circles today. And I'm not talking about emotional bosh when I talk about love; I'm talking about a strong, demanding love. For I have seen too much hate. I've seen too much hate on the faces of sheriffs in the South. I've seen hate on the

faces of too many Klansmen and too many White
Citizens Councilors in the South to want to hate,
myself, because every time I see it, I know that it
does something to their faces and their personalities,
and I say to myself that hate is too great a burden to
bear. I have decided to love. If you are seeking the
highest good, I think you can find it through love.
And the beautiful thing is that we aren't moving
wrong when we do it, because John was right, God is
love. He who hates does not know God, but he who
loves has the key that unlocks the door to the
meaning of ultimate reality...[257]

Today, in continuing to reflect on King's probing
question, "Where do we go from here?", indeed, in many
ways, the question remains yet unanswered, but is still
critical to the future. We can affirm that the distance the
church and society have traveled since 1967 in terms of race,
intercultural and inter-religious relations, gender parity,
economic justice and other human concerns has been
considerable in many ways. Most of us today can eat
wherever want to eat, shop where we want to shop, live
where we want to live, and travel and stay where we want to
stay. So the short and hopeful response to King's question,
"Where do we go from here?", could be that despite the
distance we've traveled, and despite the real and significant
challenges that remain with us as a nation and a world, and
the distance that we have yet to travel - especially as it
regards expanding opportunities for those who have the least
and who are left out among us - based on how far we've

come, remains that we can and must continue striving towards realizing the *Beloved Community.*

### Retracing the Steps of Freedom: The Pilgrimage towards the Beloved Community Today

Since 2006, I have had the opportunity to lead and teach over 150 graduate seminary students from several theological institutions in the study of the Civil Rights movement, nonviolence, peacemaking, community-building and *Beloved Community* in Alabama and across other parts of the southern United States.

These study groups usually range in size from 15-30 students, and in Alabama, we travel through Birmingham, Montgomery and Selma retracing the steps of those who participated in the American Civil Rights movement in the 1950s and 60s. Our groups are invariably very diverse. We are typically women and men, Whites, Caribbeans, Native Americans, Hispanics, Asians, Africans, Europeans and African Americans. We are typically from several different Christian denominations: United Methodist, Baptist, African Methodist Episcopal, African Methodist Episcopal Zion, Episcopalian, Lutheran, Roman Catholic, United Church of Christ, along with Muslims and others.

As we retrace the steps of freedom, we begin each day with singing, praying and reading Scripture, as was the practice in the tradition of those who participated in the American Civil Rights movement. John Lewis, now a United States Congressman from Georgia, and one of the persons who labored on the front lines of the Civil Rights movement in the 1960s, has intimated that "We never went out without singing and praying." So before leaving each morning, those of us on these immersion study trips pray, read Scripture, and sing freedom songs like "Oh Freedom," "We Shall Overcome," "There is a Balm" and "Ain't Gonna Let Nobody Turn Me Around".

As we travel - struggling through many of the difficult paths and realities of those who lived the Civil Rights movement - we invariably sense among ourselves the real possibility that culturally inclusive community – the *Beloved Community* – can indeed be realized in our lifetime.

We visit and study at numerous sites that were significant to the Civil Rights movement. In Montgomery, we visit Dexter Avenue King Memorial Baptist Church, where Rev. Dr. Martin Luther King, Jr. served as pastor from 1954-1960 at the height of the Montgomery Bus Boycott and other significant Civil Rights events. Just two blocks from Dexter Avenue Church, we visit the first Confederate White House - the home of Jefferson Davis, the president of the Confederacy. Sitting between Dexter Avenue Church and the first Confederate White House is the Alabama State Capitol – the place where Governor George Wallace and other state officials defiantly stood and spoke against any efforts toward integration and equal rights among the races, and where Wallace notoriously exclaimed, *"Segregation now, segregation tomorrow, segregation forever."* In Montgomery, we also visit the Equal Justice Initiative and the National Memorial of Peace and Justice, and learn of the legacy of lynching across America, as well as instances of modern injustice like mass incarceration, and other human rights violations around the world. And we also visit the Southern Poverty Law Center, which among other programs and activities, tracks hate-related activity and groups across America and the world.

In Birmingham, one of the places we visit is the Sixteenth Street Baptist Church, which on September 15, 1963 was bombed by segregationists, and where four Black girls (ages 11-14) were killed in the church basement while preparing for their Children's Day worship celebration. Across the street from the Sixteenth Street Baptist Church is Kelly Ingram Park, where many of the protest marches in the city of Birmingham began, and which became notorious for the atrocious and brutal acts of Police Commissioner Eugene "Bull" Connor and the Birmingham city police as they turned dogs and fire hoses on Black children of Birmingham. We visit the site of the Birmingham City Jail, where King was imprisoned, and on April 16, 1963 wrote his now-famous Letter from Birmingham Jail. Near Birmingham, we also visit Bethel Baptist Church, where Civil Rights icon, Rev. Fred Shuttlesworth served as pastor, and whose church and parsonage were bombed by segregationists on numerous occasions at the height of the Civil Rights movement in the 1950s and 60s.

In Selma, we walk across the Edmund Pettus Bridge, which was the site of "Bloody Sunday" on March 7, 1965 - when hundreds of blacks and some whites gathered in an effort to cross the bridge in a march towards Montgomery to demand voting rights, only to be violently tear-gassed, cattle-prodded, bloodily beaten and turned back by state and local authorities.    In Selma, we also visit Brown Chapel African Methodist Episcopal Church, the church where over 600 persons gathered to sing, pray, strategize and receive marching orders in their ongoing efforts to take the 54-mile journey from Selma to Montgomery.

At the conclusion of these immersion study experiences in Alabama – what we have deemed to be pilgrimages – we have been invariably struck by how far we as a society have come, and yet how far we must go.   We realize that it would not have been possible 50-60 years ago for 15-30 ministers/scholars from diverse backgrounds to travel in relative peace and safety throughout Alabama, or many other parts of the southern United States.   Furthermore, we realize that all of us – women, men, Asian, Native American and Latinx, white and black - either had, or were likely to obtain master's and doctoral degrees from major theological schools, and that this would not have been a realistic prospect 50 years ago.

Each time we journey, my memory harkens back to one of our earliest trips, where Eileen Guenther, a retired professor at Wesley Theological Seminary, who was a part of that study group, offered that it was a spiritual sung by many choirs, "I'm Gonna Sit at the Welcome Table," that played in her head throughout our experience.[258]   These tables are –

- *Lunch counters of restaurants where all had not been welcome (in the past);*

- The dining room table in the parsonage of Dexter Avenue Baptist Church, in Montgomery, where we were told, the Southern Christian Leadership Conference was formed;

- The kitchen table of the same parsonage where Dr. King searched his soul and felt God telling him to press on with his work;[259]

- The tables at which the people at Sixteenth Street Baptist Church served us lunch, tables placed adjacent to the site of the tragic bombing in September 1963 that killed four young girls;

- The tables around which members of our group gathered to share stories as victims of discrimination, of their courageous work in the Civil Rights movement (and other freedom and human rights movements), and their lament over a lack of awareness of what was going on at that time in America's history;

- Tables around which we laughed and cried together – celebrating how far we've come, yet realizing the pain inflicted upon those who made it possible for us to be able to sit at table together in light of those things that could yet still be in place to divide us.

As we've journeyed, we've also recognized that there is hope for the church and society in the fact that largely because of the heroic efforts of persons in places like Montgomery, Birmingham and Selma, Alabama; Jackson, Mississippi;

Atlanta and Augusta, Georgia; Little Rock, Arkansas; and Memphis, Tennessee - the Civil Rights Act was passed by Congress in 1964, and the Voting Rights Act and Immigration and Nationality Act were enacted in 1965, and were each signed into law by a U.S. president who was a son of the American South, Lyndon Baines Johnson.

## Martin Luther King, Jr. and the 21ˢᵗ Century Quest for the Beloved Community

In the final analysis, what Martin Luther King, Jr. advocated for when he spoke of the Christian love-ethic and the dream for a better world was the *Beloved Community*. It is in many ways counter-culturally revolutionary. With the state of the world and the churches today, we're then left to wonder what King might have to say about where we find ourselves today, and where we might be headed in the future.

In King's work, along with that of the likes of Josiah Royce, Howard Thurman and Desmond Tutu, several features of *Beloved Community* can be identified. In summary, the six features explicated here might serve to help interpret what the *Beloved Community* could look like and how it might be appropriated into the 21ˢᵗ century and beyond.

**First, the Beloved Community is rooted in the biblical notion of Agape (God's unconditional love), and is to be the ultimate goal for society and for all of creation.** King's perspective on the Christian love-ethic provides critical insight into understanding his persistent search for the *Beloved Community*. *Agape*, according to him, is the love of God operating in the human heart, and seeks to "preserve and create community." The *Beloved Community* affirms the efficacy of the Gandhian notion of *Satyagraha* (soul force) as the most effective way to enact real change in human hearts, and build authentic, radically inclusive community. The corollary Hindu principle, *ahimsa* (non-injury) is an expression and living out of the Christian love-ethic and *agape*. King stated, "We must rise to the majestic heights of meeting physical force with soul force (*Satyagraha*)."

Josiah Young asserts that for King, *agape* is the only viable alternative to deadly violence... *Agape*, (King) argues, is an active self-sacrificing devotion to peace *with* justice for all people all over the world. But *agape* is not "sentimental or affectionate emotion." It has nothing to do with the love of one's oppressors "in an affectionate sense." *Agape,* rather, is "redemptive goodwill" that purges one of enmity toward others, even if they are in fact one's nemeses.[260]

In the *Beloved Community*, power is always expressed within the context of love. According to King, "Power without love is reckless and abusive, and love without power is sentimental and anemic. Power at its best is love implementing the demands of justice, and justice at its best is power correcting everything that stands against love." [261]

***Second, the Beloved Community recognizes and honors the image of God in every human being.*** It understands that everybody is somebody, and offers radical hospitality and inclusivity to everyone as a part of God's family, the "World House". It exhibits true respect and validation of others. King insisted that we are all somebody and have dignity in God's sight. He stated, "I want to suggest some of the things that should begin your life's blueprint. Number one... should be a deep belief in your own dignity. Your worth and your own somebodiness... always feel that you count. Always feel that you have worth, and always feel that your life has ultimate significance."[262]

Richard Wills, in *Martin Luther King, Jr. and the Image of God* asserts that (King's) use of *imago Dei* language existed on the edge of a historical dialogue and quest for human and civil rights, and must therefore be viewed from within the rich traditional context from which he spoke and acted.[263] Wills further asserts that as King imagined God and contemplated what it meant to have been created in the image of God, his questions and conclusions were undeniably diffused through the lens of his personal social experience and the historical attachments that defined it.[264]

Thus, there is a reminder in King's conception of the *imago Dei* of the inherent worth and dignity of all people, and what he referred to as the "somebodiness" of all of humanity. Garth Baker-Fletcher posits that in King's theory of human dignity, he consistently pointed to the *fundamental nature of humanity*, that we have all been created by the same God, and that God loves all of that which has been divinely created. Baker-Fletcher further asserts that King's philosophy and practice reveals three qualities pertaining to human dignity: (1) dignity for King is a necessary and inherent human condition or state, (2) dignity is an exalted or elevated state of humanity achieved through courageous protest, and (3) the protest for dignity will engender a higher sense of dignity for 'civilization'.[265]

The *Beloved Community* recognizes and honors the image of God and human dignity extant in every human being. Amidst human diversity, the *Beloved Community* insists that there must be a comprehension and affirmation of the intrinsic worth in and of all persons. The apostle Paul stated, *"There is neither Jew or Greek, there is neither bond or free, there is neither male or female; for you are all one in Christ Jesus"* (Galatians 3:28).

In a world that is plagued with brokenness, separation, suspicion and deadly conflicts along racial, tribal and ethnic lines, it remains the urgent calling of Christians to affirm that God created all persons in God's image, and that we are called to exist in peaceable, just and radically inclusive community.

***Third, the Beloved Community insists that "all life is interrelated".*** King consistently affirmed that all humanity was bound together through our common creator. Hence for him, the fundamental tenets of love, prayer, forgiveness, reconciliation and peace were to be the spiritual means of addressing extant forms of oppression and social disintegration, and moving toward realizing the *Beloved Community*. Another of his fundamental beliefs was in the kinship of all persons, and the insistence that "all life is interrelated." He believed that all life is part of a single process; all living things are interrelated; and all persons are sisters and brothers. Thus, all persons have a place in the *Beloved Community.* Because all persons are interrelated, one cannot harm another without harming oneself. He said:

> To the degree that I harm my brother, no matter what he is doing to me, to that extent I am harming myself. For example, white men often refuse federal aid to education in order to avoid giving the Negro his rights; but because all men are brothers, they cannot deny Negro children without harming themselves. Why is this? Because all men are brothers. If you harm me, you harm yourself. Love, *agape*, is the only cement that can hold this broken community together. When I am commanded to love, I am commanded to restore community, to resist injustice, and to meet the needs of my brothers.[266]

King believed that each person has certain basic rights that are rooted in the interrelatedness of all persons. He further stated:

> All this is simply to say that all life is interrelated. We are caught in an inescapable network of mutuality; tied in a single garment of destiny. Whatever affects one directly, affects all indirectly... This is the way the world is made. I didn't make it that way, but this is the interrelated structure of reality.[267]

The *Beloved Community* thus insists upon the appropriation of interdependence as the impetus towards the realization of full humanity and the actualization of full community. It is in and through the *Beloved Community* that persons discover themselves, and experience the meaning and power of living together as the family of God. It seeks to build increasing levels of trust among people across difference, and it works to overcome fear of difference and fear of others through authentic human engagement, association, valuation and a striving towards community-building and peacemaking.

**Fourth, the Beloved Community posits that ours must continue to be an active yearning for peace with justice, as ultimately expressed in reconciliation.** The *Beloved Community* righteously opposes oppression and injustice, and takes direct action against racism, poverty, violence and other forms of oppression. It is not expedient or sufficient in this day and age for any of us to just go along to get along. In King's view, true peace is always connected with justice. The *Beloved Community* insists on *seeking peace and pursuing it* (Psalm 34:14), and that we must ultimately strive to realize the sentiments of the ancient prophet Amos that *"justice [would] roll down as waters, and righteousness as a mighty stream"* (Amos 5:24).

In King's conception of the *Beloved Community*, faith and action were interrelated. In this regard, theology and ethics were inextricably connected. Theology – what we believe and comprehend about God (how we talk about God)

- could not be separated from ethics – how we behave as the human family. Our creeds and our deeds have to be in concert. Our talk and our walk have to correspond. King stated in 1967, "Let us be dissatisfied until America will no longer have a high blood pressure of creeds and an anemia of deeds."[268]

This faith-action (creed-deed) dialectic found its ultimate expression in the notion of the *Beloved Community*. For King, there were essentially two steps involved in the movement towards the *Beloved Community*. First, *desegregation* would lead to the removal of legal barriers to equality. But *desegregation* was a short-term goal – and it alone was not enough. Desegregation had to be followed by *integration*.

As King defined it, *integration* is "the positive acceptance of desegregation and the welcomed participation of Negroes into the total range of human activities"[269] He further defined *integration* as genuine inter-group, interpersonal living. *Integration* advocated and facilitated the inclusion of all persons in a just society. It was the long-term goal as a means towards realizing the vision of the *Beloved Community*.

The *Beloved Community,* for King, is thus to be an integrated community in which persons of all races and creeds live together harmoniously as sisters and brothers in peace with justice. It is a product of love, and is to look like people of all races, religions and creeds dwelling together in unity. It is to be a reality where all have enough to eat, clean water to drink, and a place to live, and where true peace with justice exists. He believed that the church of Jesus Christ should be a witness to reconciliation, integration, and the *Beloved Community* in and for the world.

*Fifth, the Beloved Community depends on the collaborative efforts of cross-sections of people with common interests for a just society.* The work for peace, righteousness and justice is not to be confined to any one group of people. It is not merely the work of Blacks or Whites, Christians, Jews or Muslims, left or right, conservatives, moderates or liberals, or any other particular group - but the work for righteousness, justice and peace belongs to each and every one of us.

The sentiments of King's friend Rabbi Abraham Joshua Heschel resonate:

Morally speaking, there is no limit to the concern one must feel for the suffering of human beings; indifference to evil is worse than evil itself, and in a free society, some are guilty, but all are responsible.[270]

Archbishop Desmond Tutu stated "If you are neutral in situations of injustice, you have chosen the side of the oppressor."[271]

As King asserted at Mason Temple Church of God in Christ on April 3, 1968, we should remain cognizant that there is a certain collective force among those of us who are committed to living the sentiments of the prophet Micah to *"love kindness, do justice and walk humbly with God"*

(Micah 6:8). King said, "For when people get caught up with that which is right, and they are willing to sacrifice for it, there is no stopping point short of victory."

**Sixth, the Beloved Community beckons humanity to never give up hoping.** King died abiding in the hope of the *Beloved Community*. At his acceptance speech for the Nobel Peace Prize in 1964, he intimated what hope was to look like amidst despair:

> But with patient and firm determination we will press on until every valley of despair is exalted to new peaks of hope, until every mountain of pride and irrationality is made low by the leveling process of humility and compassion; until the rough places of injustice are transformed into a smooth plane of equality of opportunity; and until the crooked places of prejudice are transformed by the straightening process of bright-eyed wisdom.[272]

Regarding hope, Walter Brueggemann states in *A Gospel of Hope* that "Hope is the deep religious conviction that God has not quit."[273] Hope in the gospel faith is not just a vague feeling that things will work out, for it is evident that things will not just work out. Rather, hope is the conviction, against a great deal of data, that God is tenacious and persistent in overcoming the deathliness of the world, that God intends joy and peace.[274]

In *The Prophetic Imagination*, Brueggemann posits that the task of prophetic imagination and ministry is to bring to public expression those very hopes and yearnings that have been denied so long and suppressed so deeply that we no longer know they are there.[275] He asserts:

> Hope, on one hand, is an absurdity too embarrassing to speak about, for it flies in the face of all those claims we have been told are facts. Hope is the refusal to accept the reading of reality which is the majority opinion; and one does that only at great political and existential risk. On the other hand, hope is subversive, for it limits the grandiose pretension of the present, daring to announce that the present to which we have all made commitments is now called into question.[276]

Although segregation indeed continues to be pervasive and persistent in many churches (as it does in many other sectors of society), there is hope. Charles Marsh, in his book, *The Beloved Community: How Faith Shapes Social Justice, from the Civil Rights Movement to Today,* intimates that "Eleven o'clock Sunday may be the most segregated hour of the week as far as any particular parish goes, but it is the most integrated hour of the week as far as the kingdom goes."[277]

Indeed, our ultimate hope lies in building community now that will be ultimately realized in an eschatological future that is beyond this present day. Once again Marsh writes:

The hope that we must nurture is the hope that all will be made whole in the history of redemption and that together we will join hands and learn to live in the sobering light of God's promise.[278]

The *Beloved Community* is eschatological in its ultimacy in that it must continue until it is realized as the hope of creation, the actualization of God's will. Thus, the reminder again is that the teleological dream that King shared with the world in 1963 is a dream that is still applicable for us today.

### *Martin Luther King, Jr. and Creative Altruism*

King stated, "Every man must decide whether he will walk in the light of creative altruism or in the darkness of destructive selfishness." At Mason Temple Church of God in Christ in Memphis, Tennessee, on April 3, 1968, on the night before his assassination, in what has come to be known as the *"I've Been to the Mountaintop"* speech, King effectively reiterated his hope for a racially, economically and socially inclusive and just society.

To paint a picture of where society found itself, in his 41-minute set of remarks that night King recounted the story of the Good Samaritan, and offered a depiction of the Jericho road (Luke 10:25-37). He said, that the "Jericho road is a dangerous road … It's a winding, meandering road."

*But wanting to justify himself, the Pharisee asked Jesus, "And who is my neighbor?" (Luke 10:29)*

King offered insight into what it means to abide on the various Jericho roads that we must travel. He asserted that Jesus, in the parable of the Good Samaritan, disclosed his definition of a neighbor. A neighbor is Jew and Gentile; she/he is Russian and American; he/she is Muslim, Hindu, Buddhist and Christian; she/he is Native American, Hispanic and Asian, white and black. She/he is richer and poorer – left and right – conservative and liberal – Democratic, Republican and Independent, gay, lesbian and straight. A neighbor is "any certain man or woman" – any person in need – on any of the numerous Jericho roads of life.

King indicated that Jesus revealed the meaning of creative altruism as seen in the Good Samaritan who was moved by compassion to care for "a certain man" who had been robbed and beaten on the Jericho road. For King, true compassion must always be coupled with justice, and it challenges each of us in the church and society to move towards engaging in what he called forms of "creative altruism." This is altruism that makes concern for others the first law of life.

He observed that the Samaritan depicted by Jesus in the Lukan text shared altruistic concern for his neighbor, and then King offered insight on what it means to show altruistic concern on the various Jericho roads that persons must travel today. He pointed out that the creative altruism that the Good Samaritan demonstrated was *universal, excessive and dangerous.*

Today, King might remind us that the most important expression of this type of *universal, excessive and dangerous* altruism is how we raise our children, and work to secure their future. Why is this important?

Marion Wright Edelman, of the Children's Defense Fund, stated:

> We are at risk of letting our children drown in the bathwater of American materialism, greed and violence. We must regain our spiritual bearings and roots and help America recover hers before millions more children – Black, Brown and White, poor, middle-class and rich – self-destruct or grow up thinking life is about acquiring rather than sharing, selfishness rather than sacrifice, and material rather than spiritual wealth. And even as so much progress has been made, for too many Black children and families, progress is not coming quickly enough or at all.[279]

Edelman continues. Consider these statistics about Black children living in the U.S.:

- Every five seconds during the school day, a Black public school student is suspended.
- Every forty-six seconds during the school day, a Black high school student drops out.
- Every minute, a Black child is arrested and a Black baby is born to an unmarried mother.
- Every three minutes, a Black child is born into poverty.

- Every hour a Black baby dies.
- Every four hours a Black child or youth under twenty dies from an accident.
- Every five hours a Black child or youth under twenty is a homicide victim.
- Every day, a Black young person under twenty-five dies from HIV infection.
- Every day, a Black child or youth under twenty commits suicide.

Edelman further intimates that we must learn to reweave the rich fabric of community for our children and to re-install the values and sense of purpose our elders and mentors have always embraced... A massive new movement must well up from every nook, cranny, and place in our community involving millions of parents; religious, civic, educational, business, and political leaders; and youths themselves.[280]

Indeed, the plight of our collective morality is seen in the ways that our children are treated. Dietrich Bonhoeffer is commonly attributed with intimating that "the test of the morality of a society is what it does for its children." According to Edelman, based on the statistics above, the United States is failing Bonhoeffer's test every day. Thus, King might remind us that creative altruism and justice can and must begin with assuring that all children of the world are fully educated, fed, housed, clothed and protected.

Creative altruism that is *universal, dangerous and excessive* ultimately involves extending compassionate acts to all of our sisters and brothers. In his sermon "Beyond

Vietnam: A Time to Break Silence", preached at Riverside
Church in New York on April 4, 1967, King stated:

> Here is the true meaning and value of compassion
> and nonviolence when it helps us see the enemy's
> point of view, to hear his questions, to know his
> assessment of ourselves. For from his view we may
> indeed see the basic weaknesses of our own
> condition, and if we are mature, we may learn and
> grow and profit from the wisdom of the brothers who
> are called the opposition.[281]

When such creative altruism is practiced, we are led
to not only offer a handout, but we ask why people need a
handout in the first place. Such creative altruism, according
to King, not only offers help to the beggar, to the stripped
and robbed among us, but questions the conditions that lead
to poverty and violence – people being stripped and robbed -
in the first place. He stated, that "true compassion is more
than flinging a coin to a beggar; it is not haphazard and
superficial. It comes to see that an edifice which produces
beggars needs restructuring."

Michael Eric Dyson points out that King believed
that charity was a poor substitute for justice. Charity alone is
a hit-or-miss proposition; people who tire of giving stop
doing so when they think they've done enough. Justice
seeks to take the distracting and fleeting emotions out of
giving. Justice does not depend on feeling to do the right
thing. Justice depends on right action and sound thinking
about the most helpful route to the best and most virtuous
outcome. King understood and embodied this noble

distinction. People who give money to the poor deserve praise; people who give their lives to the poor deserve honor.[282]

### *"I've Seen the Promised Land"*

At his assassination, Martin Luther King, Jr. was in Memphis to advocate for the rights of striking sanitation workers. This is not coincidental in that one of the pillars of his insistent striving towards justice and the *Beloved Community* in America was for addressing *economic inequality* – along with what he deemed to be the concomitant triplets of evil - *racism and militarism*.

In his last book, *Where Do We Go from Here?*, King offered the alarming, haunting assertion, "Over the bleached bones of jumbled residues of numerous civilizations are written the pathetic words: "Too late."[283] We are "confronted with the *fierce urgency of now*, the time to think and act nonviolently."[284]

Indeed, the fierce sense of urgency that King wrote and spoke of at various points in his ministry was felt then across the nation, and much progress was eventuated in America up to his assassination on a balcony at the Lorraine Motel in Memphis at 6:01 pm on April 4, 1968. This progress, again, was clearly seen in the passage of national Civil Rights, Voting Rights and Immigration/Nationality legislation in 1964 and 1965, and this progress seemed to come to full fruition with the election of Barack H. Obama as the 44<sup>th</sup> President of the United States on November 11, 2008.

And yet, subsequent years have seen the heightened emergence (or re-emergence) of evils such as racism, classism, sexism, misogyny, homophobia, Islamophobia, xenophobia, anti-immigration, war and terror, and other spiritual and social maladies that have served to perpetuate division throughout much of society, and even throughout large segments of the churches.

Toward the conclusion of his remarks at Mason Temple, King prophetically declared, *"Well, I don't know what will happen now; we've got some difficult days ahead. But it really doesn't matter with me now, because I've been to the mountaintop... I've looked over, and I've seen the promised land. I may not get there with you, but I want you to know tonight that we as a people will get to the promised land. So I'm happy tonight. I'm not worried about anything. I'm not fearing any man. Mine eyes have seen the glory of the coming of the Lord."*

These were Martin Luther King, Jr.'s final public words.

### Conclusion

Rev. Dr. Martin Luther King, Jr. was a Christian minister, public theologian and prophetic leader, called by God to place before the church and the world the divine imperative of the *Beloved Community*. He viewed the *Beloved Community* as the most meaningful communal expression of God's will, which was revealed in the life, mission and message of Jesus of Nazareth.

Through his analysis, integration and appropriation of various strands of theological, philosophical and socio-political thinking, King arrived at a praxiological synthesis and articulation of the relationship among love, peace, justice, forgiveness, righteousness, redemption and power, with particular focus on devising nonviolent, peaceful means of eradicating oppression on the basis of race, class, and other forms of social distinction and disembodiment in the American churches and society. His persistent objective was to raise the moral conscience of society and the churches, and to move the nation and the world towards the actualization of the *Beloved Community.*

In the final analysis, King went to great lengths to explicate the quality of whole-hearted, profound Christian love, *agape,* which can and must be the substance uniting all humanity into a common bond of sisters and brothers, showing forth in all human relationships, and ultimately being expressed in the realization of the *Beloved Community.*

Although segregation indeed continues to abound in many churches, as well as in many other sectors of society, there is hope. Thus, we must never give up hoping. A part of the dream that Rev. Dr. Martin Luther King, Jr. shared with the world on the steps of the Lincoln Memorial in August 1963 (that I believe still holds today) was, again, that there would be "[hewn] out of the mountain of despair, a stone of hope."

We must never stop imagining and dreaming of the *"future with hope"* (Jeremiah 29:11) that is God's will for the churches and the world. This is the essence of hope and striving for the *Beloved Community.*

## *ENDNOTES*

### Introduction Notes

[1] Kenneth Smith and Ira Zepp, Jr., *Search for the Beloved Community: The Thinking of Martin Luther King, Jr.* (Valley Forge, PA: Judson Press, 1974, 1998), see pp. 129-156.
[2] Smith and Zepp, *Search for the Beloved Community*, 130.
[3] Walter Earl Fluker, *They Looked for a City: A Comparative Analysis of the Ideal of Community in the Thought of Howard Thurman and Martin Luther King, Jr.* (New York: University Press of America, 1989), 110.

### Chapter Two Notes

[4] Lewis V. Baldwin, *There is a Balm: The Cultural Roots of Martin Luther King, Jr.* (Minneapolis, MN: Fortress Press, 1991), 3.
[5] Baldwin, *There is a Balm*, 3.
[6] Robert L. Franklin, *Liberating Visions: Human Fulfillment and Social Justice in African-American Thought* (Minneapolis: Fortress Press, 1990), 105.
[7] Clayborne Carson, "Martin Luther King, Jr. and the African-American Social Gospel" in *African-American Religion: Interpretive Essays in History and Culture,* Timothy Fulop and Albert Raboteau, eds. (New York: Routledge, 1997), pp. 345-6.
[8] Franklin, *Liberating Visions*, 106.
[9] Stephen B. Oates, *Let the Trumpet Sound* (New York: HarperPerennial, 1982), 10.
[10] Oates, *Let the Trumpet Sound,* 10.

[11] Carson, "Martin Luther King, Jr. and the African-American Social Gospel", 349. Carson makes reference to King's paper, "Autobiography of Religious Development," *Papers of Martin Luther King, Jr., Volume I,* Clayborne Carson, ed. (Berkley, CA: University of California Press, 1992), 361.

[12] Martin Luther King, Jr. "The Un-Christian Christian," *Ebony Magazine* (Chicago: Johnson Publishing, August 1965), 76.

[13] Carson, "Martin Luther King, Jr. and the African-American Social Gospel", 344.

[14] Carson, "Martin Luther King, Jr. and the African-American Social Gospel", 344.

[15] Smith and Zepp, *Search for the Beloved Community,* 3. Here, Smith and Zepp make reference to a speech made by King to the American Baptist Convention shortly before the start of the Montgomery Bus Boycott.

[16] Carson, "Martin Luther King, Jr. and the African-American Social Gospel", 351.

[17] Carson, "Martin Luther King, Jr. and the African-American Social Gospel", 347.

[18] Mark L. Chapman, *Christianity on Trial: African-American Religious Thought Before and After Black Power* (Maryknoll, NY: Orbis Books, 1996), 27.

[19] Chapman, *Christianity on Trial,* 16. Here, Chapman makes reference to Keith D. Miller's landmark study of King's language and its sources. See also Keith D. Miller, *Voice of Deliverance: The Language of Martin Luther King, Jr., and Its Sources* (New York: The Free Press, 1992), 44.

[20] Chapman, *Christianity on Trial,* 15.

[21] Chapman, *Christianity on Trial,* 15.

[22] Cornel West, *Prophetic Fragments: Illuminations of the Crisis in American Religion and Culture* (Grand Rapids, MI: Eerdmans, 1988), pp. 271-272, West alludes to Italian

philosopher Antonio Gramsci's distinction between "organic" and "traditional" intellectuals, as fully explicated in Gramsci's *Prison Notebooks.*

[23] Smith and Zepp, *Search for the Beloved Community,* 18.

[24] Smith and Zepp, *Search for the Beloved Community,* 18.

[25] Smith and Zepp, *Search for the Beloved Community,* 18.

[26] Smith and Zepp, *Search for the Beloved Community,* 21.

[27] Smith and Zepp, *Search for the Beloved Community,* 22.

[28] Smith and Zepp, *Search for the Beloved Community,* 23.

[29] Smith and Zepp, *Search for the Beloved Community,* 20.

[30] Smith and Zepp, *Search for the Beloved Community,* 21.

[31] Franklin, *Liberating Visions,* 109.

[32] Gary Dorrien, *Breaking White Supremacy: Martin Luther King, Jr. and the Black Social Gospel* (New Haven, CT: Yale University Press, 2018), 18.

[33] Franklin, *Liberating Visions,* 109.

[34] Franklin, *Liberating Visions,* 109.

[35] Franklin, *Liberating Visions,* 109.

[36] Rufus Burrow, Jr., *Personalism: A Critical Introduction* (St. Louis, MO: Chalice Press, 1999), 32.

[37] Rufus Burrow, Jr., *God and Human Dignity: The Personalism, Theology and Ethics of Martin Luther King, Jr.* (Notre Dame, IN: University of Notre Dame Press, 2006), 69.

[38] Burrow, *God and Human Dignity,* 69.

[39] Martin Luther King, Jr., "Conceptions and Impressions of Religion," *Papers of Martin Luther King, Jr., Volume I,* Clayborne Carson, ed., pp. 415-416.

[40] Martin Luther King, Jr., *Stride toward Freedom: The Montgomery Story* (Boston: Beacon, 1958 (updated, 1986), 88.

[41] Carson, "Martin Luther King, Jr. and the American Social Gospel", 352. Here, Carson makes reference to King's perspectives on Personalism in the "Place of Reason and

Experience," *Papers of Martin Luther King, Jr., Volume I,* 234.

[42] Martin Luther King, Jr., "Three Dimensions of the Complete Life," in *Strength to Love* (New York: Harper and Row, 1963), pp. 69-73.

[43] Smith and Zepp, *Search for the Beloved Community,* 76.

[44] Smith and Zepp, *Search for the Beloved Community,* 71.

[45] See, Robert Franklin, *Liberating Visions,* 109f. Franklin points out that King, in his conception of the "Three Dimensions of the Complete Life," makes reference to Paul Tillich's *Love, Power and Justice* (London: Oxford University Press, 1954), 78.

[46] King, "Three Dimensions of the Complete Life," *Strength to Love,* pp. 69-73.

[47] Sylvie Laurent, *King and the Other America: The Poor People's Campaign and the Quest for Economic Equality* (Oakland, CA: California University Press, 2018), 68. Laurent offers an account from Martin Luther King, Jr., "Preaching Ministry", 14 September-24 November 1948 in Clayborne Carson, ed., *The Papers of Martin Luther King, Jr., Volume VI: Advocate of the Social Gospel, September 1948-March 1963* (Berkley: University of California Press, 2007), 123.

[48] Franklin, *Liberating Visions,* 107.

[49] Walter Rauschenbusch, *A Theology of the Social Gospel* (Louisville, KY: Westminster John Knox Press, 1945), 1.

[50] Dorrien, *Breaking White Supremacy,* 1.

[51] Dorrien, *Breaking White Supremacy* 2.

[52] Peter Paris, *The Social Teaching of the Black Churches* (Minneapolis: Fortress Press, 1985), see chapter 5.

[53] Smith and Zepp, *Search for the Beloved Community,* 26.

[54] Dorrien, *Breaking White Supremacy,* 18.

[55] Smith and Zepp, *Search for the Beloved Community,* 31. Smith and Zepp offer an analysis of Rauschenbusch's

perspectives on ethical and moral religion as outlined in *Christianity and the Social Crisis* (New York; Harper & Row, 1907).

[56] Smith and Zepp, *Search for the Beloved Community,* 32.

[57] Smith and Zepp, *Search for the Beloved Community,* 32.

[58] Smith and Zepp, *Search for the Beloved Community,* 33.

[59] Smith and Zepp, *Search for the Beloved Community,* 33.

[60] Martin Luther King, Jr., "A Knock at Midnight", *Strength to Love* (New York: Harper & Row, 1963), 57.

[61] Martin E. Marty, *Pilgrims in Their Own Land: 500 Years of Religion in America* (New York: Penguin Books, 1984), 441.

[62] Carson, "Martin Luther King, Jr. and the African-American Social Gospel", 354.

[63] Martin Luther King, Jr., "How Modern Christians Should Think of Man," in Carson, ed., *Papers of Martin Luther Kings, Jr., Volume I,* 273.

[64] Smith and Zepp, *Search for the Beloved Community,* 73.

[65] Reinhold Niebuhr, *Moral Man and Immoral Society* (New York: Scribner, 1933), pp. xxii-xxiii.

[66] Martin Luther King, Jr., "Reinhold Niebuhr," April 2, 1952, in *Papers of Martin Luther King, Volume II: Rediscovering Precious Values, July 1951-November 1955,* Clayborne Carson, ed.   (Berkley, CA: University of California Press, 1994), see pp 139-140.

[67] Martin Luther King, Jr., "Reinhold Niebuhr's Ethical Dualism," May 9, 1952, in  *Papers of Martin Luther King, Jr., Volume II*, see pp. 141-151.

[68] See Kenneth Smith and Ira Zepp, 73f., and Reinhold Niebuhr, *Moral Man and Immoral Society.*

[69] Carson, "Martin Luther King, Jr. and the African-American Social Gospel", 353.

[70] Smith and Zepp, *Search for the Beloved Community,* 74.

[71] Smith and Zepp, *Search for the Beloved Community,* 73.

[72] Smith and Zepp, *Search for the Beloved Community,* 88.
[73] Smith and Zepp, *Search for the Beloved Community,* 89.
[74] Niebuhr, *Moral Man and Immoral Society* , pp. 249 and 273.
[75] Reinhold Niebuhr, *An Interpretation of Christian Ethics* (New York: Harper and Brothers, 1935), 140.
[76] Carson, "Martin Luther King, Jr. and the African-American Social Gospel", 353. Here Carson makes reference to Martin Luther King, Jr., "Reinhold Niebuhr's Ethical Dualism."
[77] Martin Luther King, Jr., "My Pilgrimage to Nonviolence", *Fellowship* (New York: Fellowship of Reconciliation, September 1958).

## Chapter Three Notes

[78] Huston Smith, *The World's Religions* (San Francisco: HarperCollins, 1991), 13.
[79] E. Stanley Jones, *Gandhi: Portrayal of a Friend* (Nashville, TN: Abingdon Press, 1948), 33.
[80] Smith, *The World's Religions,* 13.
[81] See Thomas Merton, *Gandhi on Nonviolence* (New York: New Directions, 1964). Merton offers details on the life of Mohandas Gandhi.
[82] See Merton, *Gandhi and Nonviolence.*
[83] John Dear, "The Experiments of Gandhi: Nonviolence in the Nuclear Age," *Fellowship* (New York: Fellowship of Reconciliation, January/February, 1988).
[84] J. Deotis Roberts, "Gandhi and King: On Conflict Resolution," in *Shalom Papers: A Journal of Theology and Public Policy,* Victoria J. Barnett, ed. (Washington, DC: Church's Center for Theology and Public Policy,  Vol. 11, No. 2, Spring 2000), 36.

[85] Rajmohan Gandhi, "Gandhi's Unfulfilled Legacy: Prospects for Reconciliation in Racial/Ethnic Conflict," (1995 Cynthia Wedel Lecture, Church's Center for Theology and Public Policy, Wesley Theological Seminary, Washington, DC, April 27, 1995). In this lecture, Rajmohan Gandhi offers a view of Mohandas Gandhi's life and unfinished legacy from the perspective of a contemporary Indian scholar (Rajmahan Gandhi).

[86] Rajmohan Gandhi, "Gandhi; The Unfulfilled Legacy".

[87] Rajmohan Gandhi, "Gandhi; The Unfulfilled Legacy".

[88] Rajmohan Gandhi, "Gandhi; The Unfulfilled Legacy".

[89] William Shannon, *Seeds of Peace: Contemplation and Non-Violence* (New York: Crossroad Publishing, 1996), 154.

[90] Shannon, *Seeds of Peace*, 153.

[91] See Merton, *Gandhi on Nonviolence,* for details on Gandhi's development of the conceptualization of *Satyagraha.*

[92] Roberts, "Gandhi and King: On Conflict Resolution", 37.

[93] Roberts, "Gandhi and King: On Conflict Resolution", 37.

[94] Mohandas K. Gandhi, "Nonviolence – the Greatest Force," *The World Tomorrow,* (October 1926).

[95] See Dear, "The Experiments of Gandhi".

[96] See Dear, "The Experiments of Gandhi".

[97] See Dear, "The Experiments of Gandhi".

[98] Jim Wallis, *The Soul of Politics* (New York: The New Press, 1994), xiii.

[99] Shannon, *Seeds of Peace,* 154.

[100] Shannon, *Seeds of Peace,* 154.

[101] Mairead Corrigan Maguire, "Gandhi and the Ancient Wisdom of Nonviolence," *Fellowship* (New York: Fellowship of Reconciliation, June 1988).

[102] John Dear, *The Beatitudes of Peace: Meditations on the Beatitudes, Peacemaking and the Spiritual Life* (New London, CT: Twenty-Third Publications: 2016), pp. 10-12.

[103] Shannon, *Seeds of Peace,* 154.

[104] Gandhi, "Nonviolence – The Greatest Force", 124.

[105] Gandhi, "Nonviolence – The Greatest Force", 124.

[106] Dear, "The Experiments of Gandhi", pp. 10-12.

[107] Elizabeth Yates, *Howard Thurman: Portraits of a Practical Dreamer* (New York: John Day, 1964), 95.

[108] Howard Thurman, *Footprints of a Dream: The Dawn of the Idea of the Church for the Fellowship of All Peoples: Letters Between Alfred Fisk and Howard Thurman, 1943-1944* (San Francisco: Lawton and Alfred Kennedy, 1975), 24.

[109] Thurman, *Footprints of a Dream,* 24.

[110] Howard Thurman, *With Head and Heart: The Autobiography of Howard Thurman* (New York: Harcourt, Brace and Jovanovich, 1979), 132.

[111] Roberts, "Gandhi and King: On Conflict Resolution", 32.

[112] Gandhi, "Nonviolence – The Greatest Force," 124.

[113] Gandhi, "Nonviolence – The Greatest Force," 121.

[114] Gandhi, "Nonviolence – The Greatest Force," 123.

[115] Gandhi, "Nonviolence – The Greatest Force," 123. Mrs. Sue Bailey Thurman's response fits with the conceptualization of the "moral suasion" as discussed by J. Deotis Roberts. See Roberts, "Moral Suasion as Non-violent Direct Action," *Journal for Religious Thought* (Vol. 35, No. 2, Fall /Winter 1978-79), see pp. 29-43.

[116] Walter E. Fluker and Catherine Tumber eds. *A Strange Freedom: The Best of Howard Thurman on Religious Experience and Public Life* (Boston: Beacon Books, 1998), 7.

[117] Alton B., Pollard, III., *Mysticism and Social Change: The Social Witness of Howard Thurman* (New York: Lang, 1992), 37.

[118] Pollard, *Mysticism and Social Change,* 37.

[119] Pollard, *Mysticism and Social Change,* 37.

[120] Baldwin, *There is a Balm,* Baldwin offers a complete analysis of the impact of the black family and church on thinkers like Martin Luther King, Jr. and Howard Thurman in this work.

[121] King, "My Pilgrimage to Nonviolence".

[122] Roberts, "Moral Suasion as Non-violent Direct Action", 31.

[123] Roberts, "Moral Suasion as Non-violent Direct Action", 32.

[124] Roberts, "Moral Suasion as Non-violent Direct Action", 32.

[125] See Roberts, "Moral Suasion as Non-violent Direct Action", pp. 31-32.

[126] See Roberts, "Moral Suasion as Non-violent Direct Action", pp. 31-32.

[127] King, "My Pilgrimage to Nonviolence".

[128] King, *Stride toward Freedom*, 71.

[129] King, *Stride toward Freedom*, 71.

[130] Roberts, "Moral Suasion as Non-violent Direct Action", 38.

[131] Roberts, "Moral Suasion as Non-violent Direct Action", pp. 30-31. J. Deotis Roberts offers an extensive analysis of "moral suasion" in his article "Gandhi and King: On Conflict Resolution." Roberts asserts that moral suasion assumes that there are people of good will of all races.

[132] King, "My Pilgrimage to Nonviolence."

[133] King, "My Pilgrimage to Nonviolence", also in *Testament of Hope: The Essential Writings and Speeches of Martin Luther King, Jr.,* James Melvin Washington, ed., (New York: Harper Collins, 1986), 35.

## Chapter Four Notes

[134] Martin Luther King, Jr., "Beyond Vietnam – A Time to Break Silence, in *A Testament of Hope: The Essential Writings and Speeches of Martin Luther King, Jr.,* James Melvin Washington, ed. (New York: Harper Collins, 1986), 240.

[135] Taylor Branch, *The King Years: Historic Moments in the Civil Rights Movement* (New York: Simon and Schuster, 2013), pp. 5-6.

[136] James H. Cone, *Speaking the Truth: Ecumenism, Liberation and Black Theology* (Maryknoll, NY: Orbis, 1986), 37.

[137] Obery Hendricks, *The Politics of Jesus: Rediscovering the Revolutionary Nature of Jesus' Teachings and How They Have Been Corrupted* (New York: Doubleday, 2006), 5.

[138] See Hendricks, *The Politics of Jesus.* The principles are outlined and explicated upon throughout this book.

[139] Howard Thurman, *Jesus and the Disinherited* (Richmond, IN: Friends United Press, 1969), 11.

[140] Carlyle Fielding Stewart, III, *The Empowerment Church: Speaking a New Language for Church Growth* (Nashville: Abingdon Press, 2001), see pp. 23-24.

[141] Frank Thomas, *How to Preach a Dangerous Sermon* (Nashville: Abingdon Press, 2018), 45.

[142] Walter Brueggemann, *The Prophetic Imagination,* 2nd edition. (Minneapolis: Fortress Press, 2001), 65.

[143] Walter Brueggemann, *The Prophetic Imagination* (Minneapolis: Fortress Press, 1978), 80f.

[144] Brueggemann, *The Prophetic Imagination* (1978), 111.

[145] Joseph Evans, "King's Dream: Representation of the Revelation of Democratic Justice", in the American Baptist Quarterly, vol. xxxv11, Spring, 2018, no. 1, Priscilla Eppinger, ed. (Atlanta, GA: American Baptist Historical Society), pp. 52-69.

[146] Tommie Shelby and Brandon Terry, eds., *To Shape a New World: Essays on the Political Philosophy of Martin Luther King, Jr.* (Cambridge, MA: Harvard University Press, 2018), 12.

[147] Shelby and Terry, eds., *To Shape a New World,* see pp. 187-204.

[148] Martin Luther King, "Our God is Able," *Strength to Love,"* see pp.124-130 for King's complete manuscript of this sermon.

[149] King, "Our God is Able," *Strength to Love,* 124.

[150] Martin Luther King, Jr., *Where Do We Go from Here: Chaos or Community?* (Boston, MA: Beacon Press, 2010), 182.

[151] Martin Luther King, Jr., "I Have a Dream", in *A Testament of Hope: The Essential Writings and Speeches of Martin Luther King, Jr.,* James Melvin Washington, ed., 217f.

[152] King, "I Have a Dream", in *A Testament of Hope,* 217.

[153] King, "I Have a Dream", in *A Testament of Hope,* 217.

[154] King, "I Have a Dream", in *A Testament of Hope,* 217.

[155] King, "I Have a Dream", in *A Testament of Hope,* 220.

[156] Martin Luther King, Jr., "Beyond Vietnam," *Brotherman: The Odyssey of Black Men in America – An Anthology*, Herb Boyd and Robert L. Allen, eds, (New York: Ballentine, 1995), pp. 393-394.

[157] King, "Beyond Vietnam – A Time to Break Silence", in *A Testament of Hope: The Essential Writings and Speeches of Martin Luther King, Jr.,* , pp. 233-234.

[158] King, "Beyond Vietnam – A Time to Break Silence", 234.

[159] Martin Luther King, "Dr. King's Entrance into the Civil Rights Movement", audio recording where King discusses his entrance into the Civil Rights Movement, (New York: Polygram Records, 1995).

[160] Richard Lischer, *The Preacher King: Martin Luther King, Jr. and the Word that Moved America* (Oxford, UK: Oxford University Press, 1995), 174.

[161] Lischer, *The Preacher King,* 175.

[162] Lischer, *The Preacher King,* 175.

[163] See Garth Baker-Fletcher, *Somebodyness: Martin Luther King, Jr. and the Theory of Dignity* (Minneapolis: Fortress Press, 1993), 132.

[164] King, "My Pilgrimage to Nonviolence", 38.

[165] Paul Tillich, *The Courage to Be* (New Haven: Yale University Press, 1952), 1.

[166] Tillich, *The Courage to Be,* 178.

[167] Howard Thurman, *Footprints of a Dream: The Story of the Church for the Fellowship of All Peoples* (New York: Harper & Row, 1959), 7.

[168] King, *Where Do We Go from Here?,* pp. 54-55.

[169] King, *Stride toward Freedom,* 27.

[170] Cornel West, ed. *The Radical King: Martin Luther King, Jr.* (Boston: Beacon Press, 2015), 75.

[171] King, *Where Do We Go from Here?,* 202.

[172] Martin Luther King, Jr., "The Drum Major Instinct", in *A Testament of Hope: The Essential Writings and Speeches of Martin Luther King, Jr.,* 267.

## Chapter Five Notes

[173] Jim Wallis, *On God's Side: What Religion Forgets and Politics Hasn't Learned about Serving the Common Good* (Grand Rapids, MI: Brazos Press, 2013), 109.

[174] See Smith and Zepp, in *Search for the Beloved Community.* The matter of King's development of the concept of *Beloved Community* within the context of the

Christian love- ethic is explicated at various points throughout the book.

[175] Martin Luther King, Jr., in *The Christian Century,* (Chicago, IL: Christian Century, July 13, 1966).

[176] Howard Thurman, *The Search for Common Ground: An Inquiry into the Basis of Man's Experience of Community* (Richmond, Indiana: Friends United Press, 1971), pp. 2-3.

[177] Leah Gunning Francis, *Ferguson and Faith, Sparking Leadership and Awakening Community* (St. Louis, MO: Chalice, 2015), 109.

[178] See Ethnic Ministries, Board of Discipleship, *Ethnic Ministries in the United Methodist Church* (Nashville: Discipleship Resources, 1976), 1.

[179] See Ethnic Ministries, Board of Discipleship, 1.

[180] J. Philip Wogaman, *Christian Moral Judgment* (Louisville: Westminster John Knox Press, 1989), Wogaman discusses the method of positive presumption on pages 89-115.

[181] Henry Mitchell and Nicholas Cooper-Lewter, *Soul Theology: The Heart of American Black Culture* (New York: Harper and Row, 1986), 95.

[182] Mitchell and Cooper-Lewter, *Soul Theology,* 96.

[183] Mitchell and Cooper-Lewter, *Soul Theology,* 96.

[184] Wallis, *On God's Side,* see pp. 275-283.

[185] Lewis Brown Griggs and Lente-Louise Louw, *Valuing Diversity: New Tools for a New Reality,* (New York: McGraw Hill, 1995), 159.

[186] Mohandas Gandhi, *Peace: The Words and Inspiration of Mahatma Gandhi* (Boulder, CO: Blue Mountain Press, 2007), 4.

[187] Mohandas Gandhi, *Peace,* 5.

[188] Eric H. F. Law, *The Bush Was Burning but Not Consumed* (St. Louis, MO: Chalice Press, 1996), xi.

[189] Horace M. Kallen, *Cultural Pluralism and the American Idea* (Philadelphia: University of Pennsylvania Press, 1956), 55. William B. McClain in *Travelling Light* (New York: Friendship Press, 1981), pp. 99-101, offers an analysis of Kallen's thoughts on cultural pluralism.

[190] E. Stanley Jones, *Gandhi: Portrayal of a Friend.* Based on his relationship with Mohandas Gandhi, Jones offers insight on how relationships can be built across cultures and religions, with particular reference to Christianity and Hinduism.

[191] Chinua Achebe, *Things Fall Apart* (New York: Anchor Books, 1959), Achebe offers a complete exposition of the effects of western, Christian colonization upon Ibo (Nigerian) culture.

[192] Jean Marc Ela, *My Faith as an African* (Maryknoll, NY: Orbis, 1988), 91.

[193] Carolyn C. Denard, "Retrieving and Reappropriating the Values of the Black Church Tradition through Written Narratives, in *The Stones that the Builders Rejected,* Walter E. Fluker, ed. (Harrisburg, PA: Trinity Press International, 1998), 84.

[194] Jonamay Lambert and Selma Myers, *50 Activities for Diversity Training* (HRD Press, 1994) Lambert and Myers outline the process of interculturation/multiculturation in the "Path of Intercultural Learning."

[195] Bernard Haring, *The Healing Power of Peace and Nonviolence* (New York: Paulist Press, 1986), 3.

[196] Dorothee Solle, *Thinking About God: An Introduction to Theology* (Philadelphia: Trinity Press, 1990), 156.

## Chapter Six Notes

[197] Martin Luther King, Jr., "Loving Your Enemies," *Strength to Love* (Philadelphia: Fortress Press, 1981, first published in 1963), see pp. 49-57.

[198] King, *Strength to Love,* 49.

[199] King, *Strength to Love,* see pp. 50-52.

[200] King, *Strength to Love,* 52.

[201] Shannon, *Seeds of Peace,* 116.

[202] Shannon, *Seeds of Peace,* 116.

[203] Smith and Zepp, *Search for the Beloved Community,* 2.

[204] Lerone Bennett, Jr., "Eulogy of Howard Thurman: Tributes to Genius", in *The African American Pulpit* (Valley Forge, PA: Judson Press, 2001), 62.

[205] Jim Wallis, *America's Original Sin: Racism, White Privilege and the Bridge to a New America* (Grand Rapids, MI: Brazos Press, 2017), 102.

[206] Carson, "Martin Luther King, Jr. and the African-American Social Gospel", 356f.

[207] King, *Stride toward Freedom.* It is in this work that King outlines his doctrine of nonviolence. See pp. 89-95.

[208] Martin Luther King, Jr. "Suffering and Faith" *The Christian Century* (Chicago: Christian Century, April 27, 1960). See also *A Testament of Hope*, James Melvin Washington, ed., 41.

[209] Gustavo Gutierrez, *On Job: God-talk and the Suffering of the Innocent* (Maryknoll, NY: Orbis Books, 1985), 15.

[210] Viktor Frankl, *Man's Search for Meaning* (New York: Washington Square Press, 1984), 135.

[211] Elie Wiesel, *Night* (New York: Hill and Wang, 1960), In this volume Wiesel offers an account of his experience with his father in the Nazi German concentration camps in Auschwitz and Buchenwald in 1944-45.

[212] Elie Wiesel, "Days of Remembrance" remarks, Washington, DC, April, 9, 2002.

[213] Wiesel," Days of Remembrance" remarks (2002).

[214] Martin Luther King, Jr. Nobel Peace Prize acceptance speech, Oslo, Norway, December 10, 1964.

## Chapter Seven Notes

[215] Martin Luther King, Jr., "The Meaning of Hope," sermon delivered on December 10, 1967; Martin Luther King, Jr. King Center Archives, Atlanta, GA, 5ff. See also Baker-Fletcher, *Somebodyness,* 132.

[216] King, "The Meaning of Hope".

[217] Cornel West, *Hope on a Tightrope* (New York: Smiley Books, 2008), 6.

[218] Barack Obama, *The Audacity of Hope: Thoughts on Reclaiming the American Dream* (New York: Three Rivers Press, 2006), 232.

[219] King, "Beyond Vietnam – A Time to Break Silence", 238.

[220] King, "Beyond Vietnam – A Time to Break Silence", 238.

[221] King, This statement was in a speech at the University of Michigan, Ann Arbor, Michigan in 1962. King would make this assertion on several subsequent occasions.

[222] Howard Thurman, *Meditations of the Heart* (Richmond, IN: Friends United Press, 1976), 96.

[223] C. Anthony Hunt, in *The Beloved Community Toolkit* (Bel Air, MD: C. Anthony Hunt, 2018).

[224] Ta-Nehisi Coates, *Between the World and Me* (New York: Spiegel and Grau, 2015), 7.

[225] King, "The Meaning of Hope", 5. See also, Baker-Fletcher, *Somebodyness,* 132.

[226] Jürgen Moltmann, *A Theology of Hope* (Minneapolis, MN: Fortress, 1993), 25.

[227] Moltmann, *A Theology of Hope*, pp. 19-20.

[228] Moltmann, *A Theology of Hope*, 22

[229] *Songs of Zion: Supplemental Worship Resources* (Nashville: Abingdon Press, 1981), 123.

[230] King, *Where Do We Go from Here?*, see also Cornel West, ed., *The Radical King*, 80.

## Chapter Eight Notes

231 Robert F. Kennedy gave these remarks in Indianapolis, Indiana on April 4, 1968, the night Martin Luther King, Jr. was assassinated.

[232] Branch, *The King Years*, 186.

[233] Branch, *The King Years*, 186.

[234] Martin Luther King, Jr., "Letter from Birmingham Jail" in *A Testament of Hope: The Essential Writings and Speeches of Martin Luther King, Jr.,* James Melvin Washington, ed., 299.

[235] James Cone, "Theology's Great Sin: Silence in the Face of White Supremacy", in *Black Theology, 2:2* (Maryknoll, NY: Orbis, 2004), see pp. 139-152, footnote 1.

[236] Marty, 442, Martin Marty here refers to Martin Luther King Jr.'s famous "Letter from the Birmingham Jail." See also *A Testament of Hope,* James Melvin Washington, ed., pp. 296-297.

[237] Jonathan Bass, *Blessed are the Peacemakers: Martin Luther king, Jr., Eight White Religious Leaders, and the "Letter from Birmingham Jail"* (Baton Rouge, LA: Louisiana State University Press, 2001), 244.

[238] Bass, *Blessed are the Peacemakers*, 244.

[239] Kelly Brown Douglas, *Stand Your Ground: Black Bodies and the Justice of God* (Maryknoll, NY: Orbis Books, 2015), 170.

[240] Cheryl Townsend Gilkes, "The Loves and Troubles of African American Women's Bodies" in *A Troubling in My Soul,* Emilie M. Townes, ed. (Maryknoll, NY: Orbis, 1993), 232.

[241] Steven Vertovec, "Super-diversity and Its Implications," *Ethnic and Racial Studies* 30, no. 6 (2007): 1024-1054.

[242] (U.S. Census Bureau) https://www.census.gov/quickfacts/fact/table/US/PST045217 date of info 2017, date accessed August 2018.

[243] (U.S. Census Bureau) https://www.census.gov/quickfacts/fact/table/US/PST045217 date of info 2017, date accessed August 2018.

[244] (U.S. Census Bureau) https://www.census.gov/quickfacts/fact/table/US/PST045217 date of info 2017, date accessed August 2018.

[245] (U.S. Census Bureau) https://www.census.gov/quickfacts/fact/table/US/PST045217 date of info 2017, date accessed August 2018.

[246] (Pew Research Center) www.pewforum.org/religious-landscape-study/, date of info July 2015, date accessed August 2018.

[247] (Pew Research Center) www.pewforum.org/religious-landscape-study/, date of info July 2015, date accessed August 2018.

[248] Michael Emerson and Christian Smith, *Divided by Faith: Evangelical Religion and the Problem of Race,* (Oxford, UK: Oxford University Press, 2000), 154f.

[249] Emerson and Smith, *Divided by Faith*, 154f.

[250] Emerson and Smith, *Divided by Faith*, 154f.

[251] Thurman, *Jesus and the Disinherited*, pp. 11-12.

[252] Howard Thurman, *The Creative Encounter. An Interpretation of Religion and the Social Witness* (Richmond, IN: Friends United Press, 1954), 139.

[253] Martin Luther King, Jr. delivered the speech entitled "A Challenge to Social Scientists" to the American Psychological Association, in September 1967.

[254] Wallis, *America's Original Sin*, 33.

[255] See Jim Wallis, in *Sojourners* (Sojourners, November 27, 2019) and the book *Christ in Crisis: Why We Need to Reclaim Jesus* (New York: HarperCollins, 2019).

[256] Martin Luther King, Jr. delivered the speech entitled "Where Do We Go from Here: Chaos or Community?" at the 11th Annual SCLC Convention, Atlanta, Georgia, August 16, 1967.

[257] King, "Where Do We Go from Here: Chaos or Community?" (1967).

[258] See Eileen Guenther, "From the President", *The American Organist*, November 2008., vol. 42, no. 11.

[259] See King's sermon, "I Heard the Voice of Jesus Saying Still to Fight On" in *The Spiritual Autobiography of Martin Luther King, Jr.,* Clayborne Carson, ed. (New York: Warner Books, 1998), pp. 77-78.

[260] Josiah Young, "Self-Consciousness and Self-Control: Martin Luther King, Jr., A Drum Major for Nonviolence", in the *American Baptist Quarterly*, Vol. XXXII, Spring, 2018, no. 1, Priscilla Eppinger, ed. (Atlanta, GA: American Baptist Historical Society, 73. Young alludes to King's sentiments as explicated in *Stride toward Freedom*, 92.

[261] King, in "Where Do We Go from Here: Chaos or Community?" (1967).

[262] Martin Luther King, Jr., in an address at Bratt Junior High School, Philadelphia, PA, October 26, 1967.

[263] Richard Wills, *Martin Luther King, Jr. and the Image of God* (Oxford, UK: Oxford University Press, 2009), 3.

[264] Wills, *Martin Luther King, Jr. and the Image of God,* 4.

[265] Baker-Fletcher, *Somebodyness,* 30.

[266] King, "Loving Your Enemies," *Strength to Love,* pp. 41-50.

[267] King, "The American Dream," in *A Testament of Hope,* James Melvin Washington, ed., 210.

[268] King, "Where Do We Go from Here?: Chaos or Community" (1967).

[269] Smith and Zepp, *Search for the Beloved Community,* 130.

[270] Susannah Heschel, ed., *Moral Grandeur and Spiritual Audacity: Essays* (New York: Farrar, Straus and Giroux, 1996), 224. Here, Abraham Joshua Heschel is quoted.

[271] As quoted in Robert McAfee Brown, *Unexpected News: Reading the Bible with Third World Eyes* (Philadelphia: Westminster Press, 1984), 19.

[272] King, Nobel Peace Prize acceptance speech (Oslo, Norway, December 10, 1964).

[273] Walter Brueggemann, *A Gospel of Hope* (Louisville, KY: Westminster John Knox Press, 2018), 105.

[274] Brueggemann, *A Gospel of Hope,* 104.

[275] Brueggemann, *The Prophetic Imagination* (1978), 67.

[276] Brueggemann, *The Prophetic Imagination* (1978), 67.

[277] Charles Marsh, *The Beloved Community: How Faith Shapes Social Justice, from the Civil Rights Movement to Today* (New York: Basic Books, 2005), 215.

[278] Marsh, *The Beloved Community,* 215.

[279] Robert Franklin, *Crisis in the Village: Restoring Hope in African American Communities* (Minneapolis: Fortress Press, 2007), 20.

[280] Franklin, *Crisis in the Village,* 21.

[281] King, "Beyond Vietnam – A Time to Break Silence", 237.

[282] Michael Eric Dyson, *April 4, 1968: Martin Luther King, Jr.'s Death and How it Changed America* (New York: Basic Books, 2008), 210.

[283] King, *Where Do We Go From Here?*, 202.

[284] King, *Where Do We Go From Here?*, 202.

# REFERENCES AND BIBLIOGRAPHY

## Primary Works by Martin Luther King, Jr.

King, Martin Luther, Jr. "A Comparison of the Conceptions of God in the Thinking of Paul Tillich and Henry Nelson Wieman." Ph.D. Dissertation. Boston, MA: Boston University, 1955.

King, Martin Luther, Jr. "Facing the Challenge of a New Age," *Fellowship.* New York: The Fellowship of Reconciliation, February, 1957.

King, Martin Luther, Jr. *The Measure of a Man.* Philadelphia: Fortress Press, 1988.

King, Martin Luther, Jr. "My Pilgrimage to Nonviolence," *Fellowship.* New York: The Fellowship of Reconciliation, September, 1958. Also in *A Testament of Hope: The Essential Writings and Speeches of Martin Luther King, Jr.* James Melvin Washington, ed. New York: Harper Collins, 1986.

King, Martin Luther, Jr. *Strength to Love.* Philadelphia: Fortress Press, 1981 (first published in 1963).

King, Martin Luther, Jr. *Stride toward Freedom: The Montgomery Story.* Boston: Beacon, 1958 (updated, 1986).

King, Martin Luther, Jr. "Suffering and Faith," *The Christian Century.* Chicago, IL: The Christian Century, April 1960.

King, Martin Luther, Jr. *The Trumpet of Conscience.* New York: Harper & Row, 1967.

King, Martin Luther, Jr. "The Unchristian Christian," *Ebony.* Chicago: Johnson Publishing, August 1965.

King, Martin Luther, Jr. *Where Do We Go from Here: Chaos or Community?* Boston, Beacon Press, 2010.

King, Martin Luther, Jr. *Why We Can't Wait.* New York: HarperCollins, 1963.

## Secondary and Related Works

Achebe, Chinua. *Things Fall Apart.* New York: Anchor Books, 1959.

Ansbro, John J. *Martin Luther King, Jr.: The Making of a Mind.* Maryknoll, NY: Orbis Books, 1982.

Ansbro, John J. *Martin Luther King, Jr.: Nonviolent Strategies and Tactics for SocialChange.* Maryknoll, NY: Orbis Books, 2000.

Appiah, Kwame Anthony and Henry Louis Gates, eds. *Civil Rights: An A-Z Reference of the Movement that Changed America.* Philadelphia: Running Press, 2004.

Arsenault, Raymond. *Freedom Riders: 1961 and the Struggle for Racial Justice.* Oxford:Oxford University Press, 2011.

Ayres, Alex, ed. *The Wisdom of Martin Luther King, Jr.: An A-to-Z Guide to the Ideas and Ideals of the Great Civil Rights Leader.* New York: Merridian, 1993.

Baker-Fletcher, Garth. *Somebodyness: Martin Luther King, Jr. and the Theory of Dignity.* Minneapolis, MN: Fortress Press, 1993.

Baldwin, Lewis V. *Behind the Public Veil: The Humanness of Martin Luther King, Jr.*Minneapolis, MN: Fortress Press, 2016.

Baldwin, Lewis V. *In a Single Garment of Destiny: A Global Vision of Justice and Martin Luther King, Jr.* Boston: Beacon Press, 2012.

Baldwin, Lewis V. *Never to Leave Us Alone: The Prayer Life of Martin Luther King, Jr.* Minneapolis: Fortress Press, 2010.

Baldwin, Lewis V. *There is a Balm in Gilead: The Cultural Roots of Martin Luther King, Jr.* Minneapolis: Fortress Press, 1991.

Baldwin, Lewis V., ed. *"Thou Dear God": Prayers that Open Hers and Spirits – The Reverend Dr. Martin Luther King, Jr.* Boston: Beacon Press, 2012.

Baldwin, Lewis V. *To Make the Wounded Whole: The Cultural Legacy of Martin Luther King,Jr.* Minneapolis: Fortress Press, 1992.

Baldwin, Lewis V. *Toward the Beloved Community: Martin Luther King, Jr. and South Africa.* Cleveland: Pilgrim Press, 1995.

Baldwin, Lewis V. *The Voice of Conscience: The Church in the Mind of Martin Luther King, Jr.* Oxford: Oxford University Press, 2010.

Baldwin, Lewis V., Rufus Burrow, Jr., Barbara A. Holmes, and Susan Holmes Winfield. *The Legacy of Martin Luther King Jr.: The Boundaries of Law, Politics, and Religion.* Notre Dame, IN: The University of Notre Dame Press, 2002.

Barnett, Victoria J., ed. *Shalom Papers: A Journal of Theology and Public Policy*, Spring 2000, Vol. 11, No. 2. Washington, DC: Center for Theology and Public Policy, 2000.

Bass, S. Jonathan. *Blessed are the Peacemakers: Martin Luther King, Jr., Eight White Religious Leaders, and the "Letter from Birmingham Jail."* Baton Rouge, LA: Louisiana State University Press, 2001.

Battle, Michael. *Reconciliation: The UBUNTU Theology of Desmond Tutu.* Cleveland: Pilgrim Press, 1997.

Battle, Michael. *Blessed are the Peacemakers: A Christian Spirituality of Nonviolence.* Macon, GA: Mercer University Press, 2005.

Bell, Janet Dewart. *African American Women in the Civil Rights Movement: Lighting the Fires of Freedom.* New York: The New Press, 2018.

Bell, Derrick. *Silent Covenants: Brown V. Board of Education and the Unfulfilled Hopes of Racial Reform.* Oxford, UK: Oxford University Press, 2004.

Billingsley, Andrew. *Mighty Like a River: The Black Church and Social Reform.* Oxford, UK: Oxford University Press, 1999.

Bondurant, Joan V. *Conquest of Violence: The Gandhian Philosophy of Conflict.* Princeton, NJ: Princeton University Press, 1958.

Bonhoeffer, Dietrich. *The Cost of Discipleship.* New York: Macmillan Publishing Company, 1963.

Bonhoeffer, Dietrich. *Christ the Center.* Trans. Edwin H. Robertson. New York: Harper Collins, 1960.

Bonhoeffer, Dietrich. *Life Together: The Classic Exploration of Faith in Community.* Trans. John Doberstein. New York: Harper Collins, 1954.

Bonhoeffer, Dietrich. *Meditations on the Cross.* Louisville: Westminster John Knox Press, 1996.

Bonhoeffer, Dietrich. *Who is Christ for Us?* Edited and Translated by Craig Nessan and Renate Wind. Minneapolis: Fortress Press, 2002.

Boyd, Herb and Robert L. Allen, eds. *Brotherman: The Odyssey of Black Men in America – An Anthology.* New York: Ballantine Books, 1995.

Branch, Taylor. *At Canaan's Edge: America in the King Years – 1965-68.* New York: Simon and Schuster, 2006.

Branch, Taylor. *The King Years: Historic Moments in the Civil Rights Movement.* New York: Simon and Schuster, 2013.

Branch, Taylor. *Parting the Waters: America in the King Years – 1954-63.* New York: Simon and Schuster, 1988.

Branch, Taylor. *Pillar of Fire: America in the King Years – 1963-65.* New York: Simon and Schuster, 1998.

Brightman, Edgar S. *Moral Laws.* New York: Abingdon Press, 1933.

Brinkley, Douglas. *Mine Eyes Have Seen the Glory: The Life of Rosa Parks.* London: Phoenix, 2000.

Brown, Robert McAfee. *Unexpected News: Reading the Bible with Third World Eyes.* Philadelphia: Westminster Press, 1984.

Brueggemann, Walter. *A Gospel of Hope.* Louisville, KY: Westminster John Knox Press, 2018.

Brueggemann, Walter. *Living Towards a Vision: Biblical Reflections on Shalom.* New York: United Church Press, 1976.

Brueggemann, Walter. *The Prophetic Imagination.* Minneapolis: Fortress Press, 1978.

Brueggemann, Walter. *The Prophetic Imagination, 2*[nd] edition. Minneapolis: Fortress Press, 2001.

Buber, Martin. *I and Thou.* New York: Scribner's, 1958.

Burns, Stewart. *To the Mountaintop: Martin Luther King, Jr.'s Sacred Mission to Save America, 1955-1968.* New York: HarperCollins, 2004.

Burrow, Rufus, Jr. *God and Human Dignity: The Personalism, Theology and Ethics of Martin Luther King, Jr.* University of Notre Dame Press, 2006.

Burrow, Rufus, Jr. *Personalism: A Critical Introduction.* St. Louis, MO: Chalice Press, 1999.

Caldwell, Gilbert H. *Race, Racism and Reconciliation.* Philadelphia: Simon, 1989.

Carson, Clayborne, ed. *The Autobiography of Martin Luther King, Jr.* New York: Warner Books, 1998.

Carson, Clayborne. *Martin's Dream: My Journey and the Legacy of Martin Luther King, Jr.* New York: Palgrave McMillan, 2013.

Carson, Clayborne, ed. *The Papers of Martin Luther King, Jr., Volume I: Called to Serve (January 1929-June 1951).* Berkley CA: University of California Press, 1992.

Carson, Clayborne, ed. *The Papers of Martin Luther King, Jr., Volume II: Rediscovering Precious Values (July 1951-November 1955).* Berkley, CA: University of California Press, 1994.

Carson, Clayborne, ed. *The Papers of Martin Luther King, Jr., Volume III: Birth of a New Age (December 1955-December 1956).* Berkley, CA: University of California Press, 1997.

Carson, Clayborne, ed. *The Papers of Martin Luther King, Jr., Volume IV: Symbol of the Movement (January 1957-December 1958).* Berkley, CA: University of California Press, 2000.

Carson, Clayborne, ed. *The Papers of Martin Luther King, Jr., Volume V: Threshold of a New Decade (January 1959-December 1960).* Berkley, CA: University of California Press, 2005.

Carson, Clayborne, ed. *The Papers of Martin Luther King, Jr., Volume VI: Advocate of the Social Gospel (September 1948-Mach 1963).* Berkley, CA: University of California Press, 2007.

Carson, Clayborne, ed. *The Papers of Martin Luther King, Jr., Volume VII: To Save the Soul of America (January*

*1961-August 1962)*. Berkley, CA: University of
California Press, 2014.

Carson, Clayborne and Kris Shepherd, eds. *A Call to
Conscience: The Landmark Speeches of Dr. Martin
Luther King, Jr.* New York: Warner Books, 2001.

Carson, Clayborne, et. al., eds. *The Eyes on the Prize Civil
Rights Reader.* New York: Penguin Books, 1991.

Carson, Clayborne and Peter Holloran, eds. *A Knock at
Midnight: Inspiration from the Great Sermons of
Reverend Martin Luther King, Jr.* New York: Warner
Books, 2000.

Cauthen, Kenneth. *The Impact of American Religious
Liberalism.* New York: Harper & Row, 1962.

Chapman, Mark L. *Christianity on Trial: African-American
Religious Thought Before and After Black Power.*
Maryknoll, NY: Orbis Books, 1996.

Chopp, Rebecca. *The Praxis of Suffering.* Maryknoll, NY:
Orbis Books, 1986.

Coates, Ta-Nehisi. *Between the World and Me.* New York:
Spiegel and Grau, 2015.

Colaiaco, James A. *Martin Luther King, Jr: Apostle of
Militant Nonviolence.* New York: St. Martin's Press,
1993.

Collyer, Charles E. and Ira G. Zepp, Jr. *Nonviolence Origins
and Outcomes, second edition.* Victoria, BC, Canada:
Trafford Publishing, 2006.

Colston, Freddie C. *A Long Journey: Dr. Benjamin E.
Mays: Speaks on the Struggle for Social Justice in
America.* Atlanta, GA: Freddie C. Colston (Xlibris),
2011.

Cone, Cecil. *The Identity Crisis in Black Theology.*
Nashville: AMEC Press, 1975.

Cone, James H. *A Black Theology of Liberation.* New
York: J. B. Lippincott Co, 1970.

Cone, James H. *Black Theology and Black Power.* New York: Harper & Row, 1969.

Cone, James H. *The Cross and the Lynching Tree.* New York: Orbis Books, 2015.

Cone, James H. *For My People: Black Theology and the Black Church.* Maryknoll, NY: Orbis Books, 1984.

Cone, James H. *God of the Oppressed.* New York: Seabury Press, 1975.

Cone, James H. *Martin and Malcolm and America: A Dream or a Nightmare.* Maryknoll: NY: Orbis Books, 1991.

Cone, James H. *Speaking the Truth: Ecumenism, Liberation and Black Theology.* Maryknoll, NY: Orbis, 1986.

Cone, James H. *The Spirituals and the Blues.* Maryknoll, NY: Orbis, 1972.

Crawford, Vicki L., Jacqueline Anne Rouse and Barbara Woods. *Women of the Civil Rights Movement: Trailblazers and Torchbearers.* Bloomington, IN: Indiana University Press, 1990.

Curry, Michael. *The Power of Love. Sermons, Reflections and Wisdom to Lift and Inspire.* New York: Avery, 2008.

Dalton, Harlan. *Racial Healing: Confronting the Fear Between Blacks and Whites.* New York: Anchor Books, 1995.

Dash, Michael I. N., Jonathan Jackson and Stephen C. Rasor. *Hidden Wholeness: An African American Spirituality for Individuals and Communities.* Cleveland, OH: United Church Press, 1997.

Davies, Susan E. and Sister Paul Teresa Hennessee, S.A. *Ending Racism in the Church.* Cleveland, OH: United Church Press, 1998.

Dear, John. *The Beatitudes of Peace: Meditations on the Beatitudes, Peacemaking and the Spiritual Life.* New London, CT: Twenty-Third Publications, 2016.

Dear, John, ed. *Henri Nouwen: The Road to Peace.* Maryknoll, NY: Orbis Books, 1998.

Deats, Richard. *Martin Luther King, Jr.: Spirit-Led Prophet - A Biography.* New York: New York City Press, 2000.

D'Emelio, John. *Lost Prophet: The Life and Times of Bayard Rustin.* Chicago, IL: The University of Chicago Press, 2003.

DeYoung, Curtis Paul. *Coming Together: The Bible's Message in an Age of Diversity.* Valley Forge, PA: Judson Press, 1995.

Dorrien, Gary. *Breaking White Supremacy: Martin Luther King, Jr and the Black Social Gospel.* New Haven: Yale University Press, 2018.

Dorrien, Gary. *The New Abolition: W.E.B. Dubois and the Black Social Gospel.* New Haven: Yale University Press, 2015.

Douglas, Kelly Brown. *Stand Your Ground: Black Bodies and the Justice of God.* Maryknoll, NY: Orbis Press, 2015.

DuBois, W. E. B. *The Souls of Black Folk.* Chicago: A. C. McClurg & Co., 1903.

Dyson, Michael Eric. *April 4, 1968: Martin Luther King, Jr.'s Death and How it Changed America.* New York: Basic Books, 2008.

Dyson, Michael Eric. *I May Not Get There with You: The True Martin Luther King, Jr.* New York: Free Press, 2000.

Dyson, Michael Eric. *Reflecting Black: African-American Cultural Criticism.* Minneapolis: University of Minnesota Press, 1993.

Dyson, Michael Eric. *Tears We Cannot Stop: A Sermon to White America.* New York: St. Martin's Press, 2017.

Dyson, Michael Eric. *What Truth Sounds Like: RFK, James Baldwin and our Unfinished Conversation about Race in America.* New York: St. Martin's Press, 2018.

Echols, James. *I Have a Dream: Martin Luther King, Jr. and the Future of Multicultural America.* Minneapolis: Fortress Press, 2004.

Egan, Eileen. *Peace Be With You: Justified Warfare or the Way of Nonviolence.* Maryknoll, NY: Orbis Books, 1999.

Ela, Jean Marc. *My Faith as an African.* Maryknoll, NY: Orbis Books, 1988.

Ellis, Catherine and Stephen Drury Smith. *Say it Plain: A Century of Great African American Speeches.* New York: The New Press, 2005.

Ellsberg, Robert. *Gandhi on Christianity.* Maryknoll, NY: Orbis Books, 1991.

Emerson, Michael and Christian Smith. *Divided by Faith: Evangelical Religion and the Problem of Race.* Oxford, UK: Oxford University Press, 2000.

Erikson, Erik H. *Gandhi's Truth: On the Origins of Militant Nonviolence.* New York: W.W. Norton, 1969.

Erskine, Noel Leo. *King Among the Theologians.* Cleveland, OH: Pilgrim Press, 1994.

Ervin, L.D. *Step by Step: The Reverend Fred L. Shuttlesworth.* Paducah: KY: Turner Publishing Company. 1999.

Evans, James H. *We Have Been Believers: An African-American Systematic Theology.* Minneapolis: Fortress Press, 1992.

Evans, Zelia S. and J.T. Alexander, eds. *Dexter Avenue Baptist Church, 1877-1977.* Montgomery, AL: Dexter Avenue Baptist Church, 1978.

Featherstone, Mike. *Undoing Culture: Globalization, Postmodernism and Identity.* London, UK: SAGE Publications, 1995.

Felder, Cain Hope. *Troubling Biblical Waters: Race, Class and Family.* Maryknoll, NY: Orbis, 1989.

Findlay, James F., Jr. *Church People in the Struggle: The National Council of Churches and the Black Freedom Movement, 1950-1970.* Oxford: Oxford University Press, 1993.

Fischer, Louis. *Gandhi: His Life and Message for the World.* New York: Mentor Books, 1954.

Fischer, Louis, ed. *The Essential Gandhi: An Anthology of His Writings on His Life, Work and Ideas.* New York: Vintage Books, 1962.

Fitzgerald, Kelley, ed. *Racism: The Church's Unfinished Agenda – A Journal of the National United Methodist Convocation on Racism.* Washington, DC: The United Methodist Church, General Commission on Religion and Race, 1987.

Fitts, Leroy. *A History of Black Baptists.* Nashville: Boardman Press, 1985.

Fluker, Walter Earl. *Ethical Leadership: The Quest for Character, Civility, and Community.* Minneapolis: Fortress Press, 2009.

Fluker, Walter Earl, ed. *The Stones the Builders Rejected: The Development of Ethical Leadership from the Black Church Tradition.* Harrisburg, PA: Trinity Press International, 1998.

Fluker, Walter Earl. *They Looked for a City: A Comparative Analysis of the Ideal of Community in the Thought of Howard Thurman and Martin Luther King, Jr.* New York: University Press of America, 1989.

Fong, Bruce W. *Racial Equality in the Church: A Critique of the Homogeneous Unit Principle in Light of a*

*Practical Theology Perspective.* Lanham, MD: University Press of America, 1996.

Foster, Charles R. *Embracing Diversity.* Washington, DC: Alban Institute, 1997.

Foster, Charles R. and Theodore Brelsford. *We are the Church Together: Cultural Diversity in Congregational Life.* Valley Forge, PA: Trinity Press International, 1996.

Frady, Marshall. *Martin Luther King, Jr.: A Life.* New York: Penguin Books, 2002.

Francis, Leah Gunning. *Ferguson and Faith, Sparking Leadership and Awakening Community.* St. Louis, MO: Chalice, 2015.

Frankl, Victor. *Man's Search for Meaning.* Boston, MS: Beacon Press, 1959.

Franklin, John Hope and Alfred A. Moss, Jr. *From Slavery to Freedom: A History of African Americans.* New York: McGraw Hill, 1994.

Franklin, Robert M. *Another Day's Journey: Black Churches Confronting the American Crisis.* Minneapolis: Fortress Press, 1997.

Franklin, Robert M. *Liberating Visions: Human Fulfillment and Social Justice in African American Thought.* Minneapolis: Fortress Press, 1990.

Frazier, E. Franklin. *The Negro Church in America.* New York: Schocken Books, 1963.

Friedman, Leon, ed. *Brown v. Board: The Landmark Oral Argument before the Supreme Court.* New York: The New Press, 1969.

Fulop, Timothy E. and Albert J. Raboteau, eds. *African-American Religion: Interpretive Essays in History and Culture.* New York: Routledge, 1997.

Gandhi, Mohandas K. *Autobiography: The Story of My Experiments with Truth.* New York: Dover Publications, 1983.

Gandhi, Mohandas K. *Non-violence in Peace and War,* Vol. 1. Ahmedabad: Navajivan Publishing House, 1942.

Gandhi, Mohandas K. *Peace: The Words and Inspiration of Mahatma Gandhi.* Boulder, Colorado: Blue Mountain Press, 2007.

Gandhi, Mohandas K. *The Way to God.* Berkley, CA: Berkley Hills Books, 1999.

Garrow, David J. *Bearing the Cross: Martin Luther King, Jr. and the Southern Christian Leadership Conference.* New York: Quill, 1986.

Garrow, David J., ed. *The Montgomery Bus Boycott and the Women Who Started It: TheMemoir of Jo Ann Gibson Robinson.* Knoxville, TN: University of Tennessee Press, 1993.

Gates, Henry Louis and Cornel West. *The African American Century: How Black Americans Have Shaped Our Century.* New York: Free Press, 2000.

Gaustad, Edwin S., ed. *A Documentary History of Religion in America, Since 1865.* Grand Rapids, MI: Eerdmans Publishing, 1993.

Glaude, Eddie, Jr. *Democracy in Black: How Race Still Enslaves the American Soul.* Danvers, MA: Crown/Archetype, 2016.

Glisson, Susan M., ed. *The Human Tradition in the Civil Rights Movement.* Lanham, MD: Rowman and Littlefield Publishers, 2006.

Goldberg, David Theo, ed. *Multiculturalism: A Critical Reader.* Oxford, UK: Blackwell, 1994.

Gray, Cecil Conteen. *Afrocentric Thought and Praxis: An Intellectual History.* Trenton, NJ: Africa World Press, 2001.

Griggs, Lewis Brown and Lente-Louise Louw. *Valuing Diversity: New Tools for a New Reality.* New York: McGraw Hill, 1995.

Gutierrez, Gustavo. *A Theology of Liberation.* Maryknoll: NY: Orbis Books, 1971.

Gutierrez, Gustavo. *On Job: God-Talk and the Suffering of the Innocent.* Maryknoll: NY: Orbis Books, 1985.

Gutierrez, Gustavo. *We Drink from Our Own Wells: The Spiritual Journey of a People.* Maryknoll, NY: Orbis Books, 1984.

Hall, Edward T. *Beyond Culture.* New York: Doubleday, 1976.

Hall, Edward T. *The Dance of Life.* New York: Doubleday, 1983.

Hall, Edward T. *The Hidden Dimension.* New York: Doubleday, 1966.

Hall, Edward T. *The Silent Language.* New York: Doubleday, 1973.

Hansen, Drew. *The Dream: Martin Luther King, Jr., and the Speech that Inspired a Nation.* New York: HarperCollins, 2003.

Harding, Vincent. *Hope and History: Why We Must Share the Story of the Movement.* Maryknoll: NY: Orbis, 1990.

Harding, Vincent. *Martin Luther King: The Inconvenient Hero.* Maryknoll: NY: Orbis, 1996.

Harding, Vincent. *There is a River: The Black Struggle for Freedom in America.* New York: Harcourt, Brace and Co., 1981.

Haring, Bernard. *The Healing Power of Peace and Non-violence.* New York: Paulist Press, 1986.

Haskins, James. *The Life and Death of Martin Luther King, Jr.* New York: Beechtree Book, 1977.

Hendricks, Obery M. *The Politics of Jesus: Rediscovering the Revolutionary Nature of Jesus' Teachings and How*

*They Have Been Corrupted.* New York: Doubleday, 2006.

Heschel, Abraham Joshua. *Man is Not Alone: A Philosophy of Religion.* New York: Farrar, Straus and Giroux, 1951.

Heschel, Susannah, ed. *Moral Grandeur and Spiritual Audacity.* New York: Farrar, Straus and Giroux, 1997.

Honey, Michael K. *Going Down Jericho Road: The Memphis Strike, Martin Luther King's Last Campaign.* New York: W. K. Norton and Co., 2007.

Hopkins, Dwight N. *Introduction to Black Theology of Liberation.* Maryknoll: NY: Orbis, 1999.

Hopkins, Dwight N. *Shoes That Fit Our Feet: Sources for a Constructive Black Theology.* Maryknoll, NY: Orbis, 1993.

Hunt, C. Anthony. *And Yet the Melody Lingers: Essays, Sermons and Prayers on Religion and Race, vol. 1.* Lima, OH: Wyndham Hall Press, 2006.

Hunt, C. Anthony. *The Beloved Community Toolkit.* Bel Air, MD: Self Published, C. Anthony Hunt, January 2018.

Hunt, C. Anthony. *Blessed are the Peacemakers: A Theological Analysis of the Thought of Howard Thurman and Martin Luther King, Jr.* Lima: OH: Wyndham Hall Press, 2005.

Hunt, C. Anthony. *Come Go with Me: Howard Thurman and a Gospel of Radical Inclusivity.* Lima: OH: Wyndham Hall Press, 2019.

Hunt, C. Anthony. *My Hope is Built: Essays, Sermons and Prayers on Religion and Race, vol. 2.* Lima, OH: Wyndham Hall Press, 2011.

Hunt, C. Anthony. "The Search for Peaceful Community: A Comparative Analysis of the Thinking of Howard Thurman and Martin Luther King, Jr." Ph.D.

Dissertation. South Bend, IN: The Graduate Theological Foundation, 2001.

Hunt, C. Anthony. *Stones of Hopes: Essays, Sermons and Prayers on Religion and Race, vol. 3.* Lima, OH: Wyndham Hall Press, 2017.

Hunt, C. Anthony. *Upon the Rock: A Model for Ministry with African American Families.* Bristol, IN: Wyndham Hall Press, 2000.

Huntley, Horace and John W. McKerley. *Foot Soldiers for Democracy: The Men, Women and Children of the Birmingham Civil Rights Movement.* Urbana, IL: University of Illinois Press, 2009.

Huntley, Horace and David Montgomery. *Black Workers' Struggle for Equality in Birmingham.* Urbana, IL: University of Illinois Press, 2004.

Ivory, Luther D. *Toward a Theology of Radical nvolvement: The Theological Legacy of Martin Luther King, Jr.* Nashville, TN: Abingdon, 1997.

Jackson, Thomas F. *From Civil Rights to Human Rights: Martin Luther King, Jr., and the Struggle for Economic Justice.* Philadelphia, PA: University of Pennsylvania Press, 2007.

Jesudasan, Ignatius. *A Gandhian Theology of Liberation.* Maryknoll, NY: Orbis, 1984.

Johnson, Charles. *Dreamer: A Novel.* New York: Scribner, 1998.

Johnson, Charles and Bob Adelman. *King: The Photobiography of Martin Luther King, Jr.* New York: Viking Studio/Penguin Group, 2000.

Johnson, Elizabeth. *Quest for the Living God: Mapping Frontiers in the Theology of God.* New York: Bloomsbury, 2007.

Johnson, Elizabeth. *She Who Is: The Mystery of God in Feminist Theological Discourse.* New York: The Crossroad Publishing Company, 1992.

Jones, E. Stanley. *Gandhi: Portrayal of a Friend.* Nashville: Abingdon, 1948.

Jones, William R. *Is God a White Racist: A Preamble to Black Theology.* Boston: Beacon Books, 1973.

Jordan, Clarence. *The Cotton Patch Version of Matthew and John.* New York: Association Press, 1970.

Jordan, Clarence. *Sermon on the Mount.* Valley Forge, PA: Judson Press, 1952.

Kapur, Sudarshan. *Raising Up a Prophet: The African American Encounter with Gandhi.* Boston: Beacon Press, 1992.

Kelsey, George D. *Racism and the Christian Understanding of Man.* Eugene, OR: Wipf and Stock Publishers, 1965.

King, Bernice A. *Hard Questions: Heart Answers.* New York: Broadway Books, 1997.

King, Coretta Scott. *My Life with Martin Luther King, Jr.* New York: Holt, Reinhart, and Winston, 1969.

King, Dexter Scott with Ralph Wiley. *Growing Up King: An Intimate Memoir.* New York: Warner Book, 2003.

King, Preston and Walter Fluker. *Black Leaders and Ideologies in the South: Resistance and Nonviolence.* London: Routledge, 2005.

King, Preston and Walter E. Fluker, eds. *Black Leaders and Ideologies in the South: Resistance and Nonviolence.* London, UK: Taylor and Francis Ltd. *Critical Review of International Social and Political Philosophy,* Winter 2004, special issue.

Kohl, Herbert. *She Would Not Be Moved: How to Tell the Story of Rosa Parks and the Montgomery Bus Boycott.* New York: The New Press, 2005.

Kohls, L. Robert. *Developing Intercultural Awareness.* Yarmouth, ME: Intercultural Press, 1994.

Lassiter, Valentino. *Martin Luther King in the African American Preaching Tradition.* Cleveland: Pilgrim Press, 2001.

Laurent, Sylvie. *King and the Other America: The Poor People's Campaign and the Quest for Economic Equality.* Oakland, CA: University of California Press, 2018.

Law, Eric H. F. *The Bush Was Burning, But Not Consumed.* St. Louis, MO: Chalice Press, 1996.

Law, Eric H. F. *Inclusion: Making Room for Grace.* St. Louis, MO: Chalice Press, 2000.

Law, Eric H. F. *The Wolf Shall Dwell with the Lamb: A Spirituality for Leadership in a Multicultural Community.* St. Louis, MO: Chalice Press, 1993.

Lebacqz, Karen. *Justice in an Unjust World.* Minneapolis: Augsburg Publishing House, 1987.

Lee, Hak Joon. *We Will Get to the Promised Land: Martin Luther King, Jr.'s Communal-Political Spirituality.* Cleveland, OH: Pilgrim Press, 2006.

Lerner, Michael and Cornel West. *Jews and Blacks: Let the Healing Begin.* New York: Grosset Putnam, 1995.

Lewis, John and Michael D'Orso. *Walking with the Wind: A Memoir of the Movement.* New York: Harcourt, Brace and Company, 1998.

Lincoln, C. Eric. *The Black Church Since Frazier.* New York: Schocken Books, 1974.

Lincoln, C. Eric. *Coming Through the Fire: Surviving Race and Place in America.* Durham, NC: Duke University Press, 1996.

Lincoln, C. Eric. *Martin Luther King: A Profile.* New York: Hill & Wang, 1970.

Lincoln, C. Eric. *Race, Religion and the Continuing American Dilemma.* New York: Hill & Wang, 1984.

Lincoln, C. Eric and Lawrence Mamiya. *The Black Church in the African-American Experience.* Durham, NC: Duke University Press, 1990.

Ling, Peter J. *Martin Luther King, Jr.* London: Routledge, 2002.

Lingenfelter, Sherwood G. *Ministering Cross-Culturally: An Incarnational Model for Personal Relationships.* Grand Rapids, MI: Baker Books House, 1986.

Lischer, Richard. *The Preacher King: Martin Luther King, Jr. and the Word that Moved America.* Oxford, UK: Oxford University Press, 1995.

Locke, Don C. *Increasing Multicultural Understanding.* Thousand Oaks, CA: Sage Publications, 1992.

Long, Edward, L. *Peace Thinking in a Warring World: An Urgent Call for a New Approach to Peace.* Philadelphia: Westminster Press, 1983.

Long, Michael G. *Martin Luther king, Jr. on Creative Living.* St. Louis, MO: Chalice Press, 2004.

Lovin, Robin, et al. *Creating a New Community: God's People Overcoming Racism.* Nashville: Graded Press, 1989.

Lyght, Ernest S. *The Religious and Philosophical Foundations in the Thought of Martin Luther King, Jr.* New York: Vantage Press, 1972.

Lynd, Straughton and Alice Lynd, eds. *Nonviolence in America: A Documentary History.* Maryknoll, NY: Orbis, 1995.

Macquarrie, John. *Christian Unity and Christian Diversity.* London: SCM Press, 1975.

Marable, Manning. *Race, Reform, and Rebellion: The Second Reconstruction in Black America: Problems in*

*Race, Political Economy, and Society.* Boston: South
End Press, 1983.

Marsh, Charles. *The Beloved Community: How Faith
Shapes Social Justice, from the Civil Rights Movement
to Today.* New York: Basic Books, 2005.

Marsh, Charles. *God's Long Summer: Stories of Faith and
Civil Rights.* Princeton, NJ: Princeton University Press,
1997.

Marsh, Charles. *The Last Days: A Son's Story of Sin and
Segregation at the Dawn of the New South.* New York:
Basic Books, 2001.

Martinez, Elizabeth Sutherland, eds. *Letters from
Mississippi: Personal Reports from Civil Rights
Volunteers of the 1964 Freedom Summer.* Brookline,
Ma: Zephyr Press, 2002.

Marty, Martin E. *Pilgrims in Their Own Land: 500 Years of
Religion in America.* New York: Penguin Books, 1984.

Mathabane, Mark. *Kaffir Boy: The True Story of a Black
Youth's Coming of Age in Apartheid South Africa.* New
York: Plume, 1986.

Matthews, James K. *The Matchless Weapon: Satyagraha.*
Bombay, India: Bharatiya Vidya Bhavan, 1989.

Matsuoka, Fumitaka. *The Color of Faith: Building
Community in a Multicultural Society.* Cleveland, OH:
United Church Press, 1998.

Mays, Benjamin E. *Born to Rebel: An Autobiography.*
Athens, GA: University of Georgia Press, 1971.

Mbiti, John. *African Religions and Philosophy.* New York:
Anchor Books, 1970.

McAdam, Doug. *Political Process and the Development of
Black Insurgency, 1930-1970, second edition.* Chicago:
University of Chicago Press, 1982.

McClain, William B. *Black People in the United Methodist Church: Whither Thou Goest?* Nashville: Abingdon, 1990.

McClain, William B. *Travelling Light.* New York: Friendship Press, 1981.

McClendon, James William. *Biography as Theology.* Philadelphia: Trinity Press International, 1974.

McMickle, Marvin A. *Pulpit and Politics: Separation of Church and State in the Black Church.* Valley Forge, PA: Judson Press, 2014.

McMickle, Marvin A. *Where have All the Prophets Gone? Reclaiming Prophetic Preaching in America.* Cleveland, OH: Pilgrim Press, 2006.

McWhorter, Diane. *Carry Me Home: Birmingham, Alabama and the Climactic Battle of the Civil Rights Revolution.* New York: Simon and Schuster, 2001.

Merton, Thomas. *Contemplation in a World of Action.* Notre Dame, IN: University of Notre Dame Press, 1998.

Merton, Thomas. *Faith and Violence: Christian Teaching and Christian Practice.* Notre Dame, IN: University of Notre Dame Press, 1968.

Merton, Thomas. *Gandhi on Nonviolence.* New York: New Directions, 1964.

Merton, Thomas. *The Nonviolent Alternative* (Revised edition of *Thomas Merton on Peace*). New York: Farrar, Straus and Giroux, 1980.

Metzger, Bruce M. and Roland E. Murphy, eds. *The New Oxford Annotated Bible with the Apocryphal/Deuterocanonical Books (New Revised Standard Version).* New York: Oxford University Press, 1991.

Metzger, Bruce M. and Michael D. Coogan, eds. *The Oxford Companion to the Bible.* New York: Oxford University Press, 1993.

Miller, Keith D. *Voice of Deliverance: The Language of Martin Luther King, Jr., and Its Sources.* Athens GA: University of Georgia Press, 1992.

Mitchell, Henry and Nicholas Cooper-Lewter. *Soul Theology: The Heart of American Black Culture.* New York: Harper and Row, 1986.

Moldovan, Russel. *Martin Luther King, Jr.: An Oral History of His Religious Witness and His Life.* Lanham, MD: International Scholars Publication, 1999.

Moses, Greg. *Revolution of Conscience: Martin Luther King, Jr. and the Philosophy of Nonviolence.* New York: The Guilford Press, 1997.

Moyd, Olin P. *Redemption in Black Theology.* Valley Forge, PA: Judson Press, 1979.

Moltmann, Jürgen. *A Theology of Hope.* Minneapolis, MN: Fortress, 1993.

Myrdal, Gunnar. *An American Dilemma: The Negro Problem and Modern Democracy.* New York: Harper and Row, 1944.

Niebuhr, H. Richard. *Christ and Culture.* New York: Harper & Row, 1951.

Niebuhr, Reinhold. *Moral Man and Immoral Society.* New York: Scribner, 1933.

Niebuhr, Reinhold. *The Nature and Destiny of Man, Volume I: Human Nature.* New York: Scribner, 1941.

Niebuhr, Reinhold. *The Nature and Destiny of Man, Volume II: Human Destiny.* New York: Scribner, 1943.

Nouwen, Henri J. M. *The Path of Peace.* New York: Crossroad, 1995.

Nunez, Emilio A., translated by Paul E. Sywulka. *Liberation Theology.* Chicago: Moody Press, 1995.

Oates, Stephen B. *Let the Trumpet Sound: A Life of Martin Luther King, Jr.* New York: Harper Perennial, 1994.

Obama, Barack. *The Audacity of Hope: Thoughts on Reclaiming the American Dream.* New York: Three Rivers Press, 2006.

Ogletree, Charles J., Jr. *All Deliberate Speed: Reflections on the First Half-Century of Brown v. Board of Education.* New York: W. W. Norton and Company, 2004.

Panikkar, Raimundo. *The Unknown Christ in Hinduism.* Revised edition. Maryknoll, NY: Orbis Books, 1982.

Parekh, Bhikhu. *Gandhi: A Very Short Introduction.* Oxford, UK: University of Oxford Press, 1997.

Park, Andrew Sung. *Racial Conflict and Healing: An Asian-American Theological Perspective.* New York: Orbis, 1996.

Paris, Peter J. *Black Religious Leaders: Conflict and Unity.* Louisville: Westminster John Knox Press, 1991.

Paris, Peter J. *The Social Teaching of the Black Churches.* Philadelphia: Fortress Press, 1985.

Paris, Peter J. *The Spirituality of African Peoples: The Search for a Common Moral Discourse.* Minneapolis: Fortress Press, 1995.

Parr, Patrick. *The Seminarian: Martin Luther King, Jr. Comes of Age.* Chicago, IL: Lawrence Hill Books, 2018.

Paston, Amy. *Gandhi: A Photographic Story of a Life.* London: D. K. Publishing, 2006.

Peck, M. Scott. *The Different Drum: Community Making and Peace: A Spiritual Journey Toward Self-Acceptance, True Belonging and New Hope for the World.* New York: Touchstone Books, 1987.

Peck, M. Scott. *People of the Lie: The Hope for Healing Human Evil.* New York: Simon & Schuster, 1983.

Phillips, Donald T. *Martin Luther King, Jr. on Leadership.* New York: Warner Books, 1998.

Pinkney, Andrea Davis and Brian Pinkney. *Martin Rising: Requiem for a King.* New York: Scholastic Press, 2018.

Pinn, Anthony B. *The Black Church in the Post-Civil Rights Era.* Maryknoll, NY: Orbis Books, 2002.

Pollard, Alton B., III. *Mysticism and Social Change: The Social Witness of Howard Thurman.* New York: Lang, 1992.

Raboteau, Albert. *Canaan Land: A Religious History of African Americans.* Oxford, UK; Oxford University Press, 2001.

Raines, Howell. *My Soul is Rested: The Story of the Civil Rights Movement in the Deep South.* New York: Penguin Books, 1977.

Rauschenbusch, Walter. *Christianity and the Social Crisis.* New York; Harper & Row, 1907.

Rauschenbusch, Walter. *A Theology of the Social Gospel.* Louisville, KY: Westminster John Knox Press. 1954.

Recinos, Harold J. *Jesus Weeps: Global Encounters on Our Doorstep.* Nashville: Abingdon, 1992.

Recinos, Harold J. *Who Comes in the Name of the Lord: Jesus at the Margins.* Nashville: Abingdon, 1997.

Reid, Stephen Breck. *Listening In: A Multicultural Reading of the Psalms.* Nashville: Abingdon, 1997.

Rieder, Jonathan. *Gospel of Freedom: Martin Luther King, Jr.'s Letter from Birmingham Jail and the Struggle that Changed a Nation.* New York: Bloomsbury, 2014.

Rieder, Jonathan. *The Word of the Lord is Upon Me: The Righteous Performance of Martin Luther King, Jr.* Cambridge, MA: Harvard University Press, 2008.

Roberts, J. Deotis. *Africentric Christianity: A Theological Appraisal for Ministry.* Valley Forge, PA: Judson Press, 2000.

Roberts, J. Deotis. *Bonhoeffer and King: Speaking Truth to Power.* Louisville, KY: Westminster John Knox Press, 2005.

Roberts, J. Deotis. *Liberation and Reconciliation: A Black Theology.* New York: Orbis, 1994.

Roberts, J. Deotis. *The Prophethood of Black Believers: An African American Political Theology for Ministry.* Louisville, KY: Westminster John Knox Press, 1994.

Romano, Renee C. and Leigh Raiford, eds. *The Civil Rights Movement in American Memory.* Athens, GA: University of Georgia Press, 2006.

Ross, Rosetta E. *Witnessing and Testifying: Black Women, Religion and Civil Rights.* Minneapolis: Fortress Press, 2003.

Schneier, Marc. *Shared Dreams: Martin Luther King, Jr. and The Jewish Community.* Woodstock, VT: Jewish Lights, 1999.

Sernett, Milton C., ed. *Afro-American Religious History: A Documentary Witness.* Durham, NC: Duke University Press, 1985.

Shannon, William H. *Seeds of Peace: Contemplation and Non-Violence.* New York: Crossroad Publishing, 1996.

Shelby, Tommie and Brandon Terry, eds. *To Shape a New World: Essays on the Political Philosophy of Martin Luther King, Jr.* Cambridge, MA: Harvard University Press, 2018.

Shird, Kevin and Nelson Malden. *The Colored Waiting Room: Empowering the Original and New Civil Rights Movements.* New York: Apollo Publishers, 2018.

Sitkoff, Harvard. *King: Pilgrimage to the Mountaintop.* New York: Hill and Wang, 2008.

Sitkoff, Harvard. *The Struggle for Black Equality, 1954-1980.* New York: Hill and Wang, 1981.

Smiley, Tavis. *Death of a King: The Real Story of Dr. Martin Luther King, Jr.'s Final Year.* New York: Little, Brown and Company, 2014.

Smith, Huston. *The World's Religions.* New York: Harper Collins, 1991.

Smith, Kenneth L. and Ira Zepp, Jr. *Search for the Beloved Community: The Thinking of Martin Luther King, Jr.* Valley Forge, PA: Judson Press, 1974.

Smith, Kenneth L. and Ira Zepp, Jr. *Search for the Beloved Community: The Thinking of Martin Luther King, Jr. (second edition).* Valley Forge, PA: Judson Press, 1998.

Sobrino, Jon. *Spirituality of Liberation: Toward Political Holiness.* Maryknoll: Orbis Books, 1988.

Solle, Dorothee. *Suffering.* Philadelphia: Fortress Press, 1975.

Solle, Dorothee. *Thinking about God: An Introduction to Theology.* Philadelphia: Trinity Press, 1990.

*Songs of Zion (Supplemental Worship Resources),* Nashville: Abingdon Press, 1981.

Sowell, Thomas S. *Civil Rights: Rhetoric or Reality?* New York: Quill, 1984.

Sowell, Thomas S. *Race and Culture: A World View.* New York: Basic Books, 1994.

Spencer, Jon Michael. *Protest and Praise: Sacred Music of Black Religion.* Minneapolis, MN: Fortress Press, 1990.

Stanton, Mary. *From Selma to Sorrow: The Life and Death of Viola Liuzzo.* Athens, GA: University of Georgia Press, 1998.

Stassen, Glen H. *Just Peacemaking: Transforming Initiatives for Justice and Peace.* Louisville, KY: Westminster John Knox Press, 1992.

Steele, Shelby. *The Content of Our Character: A New Vision for Race in America.* New York: HarperPerennial, 1990.

Stevenson, Bryan. *Just Mercy: A Story of Justice and Redemption.* New York: Penguin Random House. 2014.

Stewart, Carlyle Fielding, III. *African-American Church Growth: 12 Principles for Prophetic Ministry.* Nashville: Abingdon, 1994.

Stewart, Carlyle Fielding, III. *Black Spirituality and Black Consciousness: Soul Force, Culture and Freedom in the African-American Experience.* Trenton, NJ: Africa World Press, 1999.

Stewart, Carlyle Fielding, III. "A Comparative Analysis of Theological-Ontological and Ethical Method in the Theologies of James H. Cone and Howard Thurman." Ph.D. Dissertation. Evanston, IL: Northwestern University, 1982.

Stewart, Carlyle Fielding, III. *The Empowerment Church: Speaking a New Language for Church Growth.* Nashville: Abingdon Press, 2001.

Stewart, Carlyle Fielding, III. *God, Being and Liberation: A Comparative Analysis of the Theologies of James Cone and Howard Thurman.* Lanham, MD: University Press, 1989.

Stewart, Carlyle Fielding, III. *Soul Survivors: An African American Spirituality.* Louisville, KY: Westminster John Knox, 1997.

Stewart, Edward C. and Milton J. Bennett. *American Cultural Patterns: A Cross-Cultural Perspective.* Yarmouth, ME, Intercultural Press, 1991.

Storti, Craig. *The Art of Crossing Cultures.* Yarmouth, ME: Intercultural Press, 1989.

Storti, Craig. *Cross-Cultural Dialogues.* Yarmouth, ME: Intercultural Press, 1994.

Sundquist, Eric J. *King's Dream.* New Haven, CT: Yale University Press, 2009.

Sutherland, Arthur. *I Was a Stranger: A Christian Theology of Hospitality.* Nashville: Abingdon Press, 2006.
Thomas, Frank A. *How to Preach a Dangerous Sermon.* Nashville: Abingdon Press, 2018.
Thomas, James S. *Methodism's Racial Dilemma: The Story of the Central Jurisdiction.* Nashville: Abingdon, 1992.
Thompson, Marjorie. *Soul Feast: An Invitation to the Christian Spiritual Life.* Louisville, KY: Westminster John Knox Press, 1995.
Thoreau, Henry David. *Civil Disobedience and Other Essays.* New York: Dover Publications, 1993.
Thurman, Howard. *The Creative Encounter. An Interpretation of Religion and the Social Witness.* Richmond, IN: Friends United Press, 1954.
Thurman, Howard. *Deep River and the Negro Spiritual Speaks of Life and Death.* Richmond, IN: Friends United Press, 1975.
Thurman, Howard. *Disciplines of the Spirit.* Richmond, IN: Friends United Press, 1963.
Thurman, Howard. *Footprints of a Dream: The Story of the Church for the Fellowship of All Peoples.* New York: Harper & Row, 1959.
Thurman, Howard. *Jesus and the Disinherited.* Richmond, IN: Friends United Press, 1969.
Thurman, Howard. *The Luminous Darkness.* Richmond, IN: Friends United Press, 1965.
Thurman, Howard. *Meditations of the Heart.* Richmond, IN: Friends United Press, 1976.
Thurman, Howard. *The Search for Common Ground: An Inquiry into the Basis of Man's Experience of Community.* Richmond, IN: Friends United Press, 1971.
Thurman, Howard. *With Head and Heart: The Autobiography of Howard Thurman.* New York: Harcourt, Brace and Jovanovich, 1979.

Thurman, Michael, ed. *Voices from the Dexter Pulpit.* Montgomery, AL: New South Books, 2007.

Tillich, Paul. *The Courage to Be.* New Haven, CT: Yale University Press, 1952.

Tillich, Paul. *Love, Power, and Justice.* London: Oxford University Press, 1954.

Tillich, Paul. *Systematic Theology, Volume I – Reason and Revelation and Being and God.* Chicago: Chicago University Press, 1951.

Tillich, Paul. *Systematic Theology, Volume II – Existence and the Christ.* Chicago: Chicago University Press, 1957.

Tillich, Paul. *Systematic Theology, Volume III – Life and the Spirit, History and the Kingdom of God.* Chicago: Chicago University Press, 1963.

Tillich, Paul. *Theology of Peace.* Louisville: Westminster/John Knox, 1990.

Townes, Emily M. *In a Blaze of Glory: Womanist Spirituality As Social Witness.* Nashville, TN: Abingdon Press, 1995.

Townes, Emily M., ed. *A Troubling in My Soul: Womanist Perspectives on Evil and Suffering.* New York: Orbis, 1993.

Townes, Emily M., ed. *Embracing the Spirit: Womanist Perspectives on Hope, Salvation and Transformation.* New York: Orbis, 1997.

Tutu, Desmond. *God has a Dream: A Vision of Hope for Our Future.* New York: Doubleday, 2004.

Tutu, Desmond. *No Future without Forgiveness.* New York: Doubleday, 1999.

Vaughn, Wally G. and Richard W. Wills, eds. *Reflections on Our Pastor: Dr. Martin Luther King, Jr. at Dexter Avenue Baptist Church (1954-1960).* Dover, MA: Majority Press, 1999.

Vivian, Octavia. *Coretta: The Story of Coretta Scott King.* Minneapolis, MN: Fortress Press, 2006.

Volf, Miroslav. *Exclusion or Embrace: A Theological Exploration of Identity, Otherness, and Reconciliation.* Nashville: Abingdon, 1996.

Volf, Miroslav. *A Public Faith: How Followers of Christ Should Serve the Common Good.* Grand Rapids, MI: Brazos Press, 2011.

Waldschmidt-Nelson, Britta. *Dreams and Nightmares: Martin Luther King, Jr., Malcolm X and the Struggle for Black Equality in America.* Gainesville, FL: University Press of Florida, 2012.

Walker, Wyatt T. *Somebody's Calling My Name: Black Sacred Music and Social Change.* Valley Forge, PA: Judson Press, 1992.

Wallis, Jim. *America's Original Sin: Racism, White Privilege and the Bridge to a New America.* Grand Rapids, MI: Brazos Press, 2017.

Wallis, Jim. *Christ in Crisis: Why We Need to Reclaim Jesus.* New York: HarperCollins, 2019.

Wallis, Jim. *God's Politics: Why the Right Gets it Wrong and the Left Doesn't Get It.* San Francisco, CA: Harper, 2005.

Wallis, Jim. *On God's Side: What Religion Forgets and Politics Hasn't Learned about Serving the Common Good.* Grand Rapids, MI: Brazos Press, 2013.

Wallis, Jim. *The Soul of Politics: Beyond the "Religious Right" and "Secular Left."* San Diego, CA: Harcourt, Brace and Company, 1994.

Wallis, Jim. *The (Un) Common Good: How the Gospel Brings Hope to the World Divided.* Grand Rapids, MI: Brazos Press, 2013.

Warnock, Raphael. *The Divided Mind of the Black Church: Theology, Piety and Public Witness.* New York: New York University Press, 2013.

Warren, Mervyn A. *King Came Preaching: The Pulpit Power of Dr. Martin Luther King, Jr.* Downers Grove, IL: InterVarsity Press, 2001.

Washington, James Melvin. *Frustrated Fellowships: The Black Baptist Quest for Social Power.* Macon: Mercer University Press, 1986.

Washington, James Melvin, ed. *A Testament of Hope: The Essential Writings and Speeches of Martin Luther King, Jr.* New York: Harper Collins, 1986.

Washington, Raleigh and Glen Kehrein. *Breaking Down Walls: A Model for Reconciliation in an Age of Racial Strife.* Chicago: Moody Press, 1993.

Watley, William D. *Roots of Resistance: The Nonviolent Ethic of Martin Luther King, Jr.* Valley Forge, PA: Judson Press, 1985.

West, Cornel. *Democracy Matters.* New York: Penguin Press, 2004.

West, Cornel. *Keeping Faith: Philosophy and Race in America.* New York: Routledge, 1993.

West, Cornel. *Hope on a Tightrope.* New York: Smiley Books, 2008.

West, Cornel. *Prophetic Fragments: Illuminations of the Crisis in American Religion and Culture.* Grand Rapids, MI: Eerdmans, 1988.

West, Cornel. *Prophetic Reflections: Notes on Race and Power in America.* Philadelphia: Westminster Press, 1982.

West, Cornel. *Prophesy Deliverance! An Afro-American Revolutionary Christianity.* Philadelphia: Westminster Press, 1982.

West, Cornel. *Race Matters.* Boston: Beacon Press, 1991.

West, Cornel, ed.. *The Radical King: Martin Luther King, Jr.* Boston: Beacon Press, 2015.

West, Russell W. "That His People May be One: An Interpretive Analysis of the Pentecostal Leadership's Quest of Racial Unity." Ph.D. Dissertation. Virginia Beach, VA: Regent University, 1998.

Wexler, Stuart and Larry Hancock. *Killing King: Racial Terrorists, James Earl Ray, and the Plot to Assassinate Martin Luther King, Jr.* Berkley, CA: Counterpoint, 2018.

White, Marjorie L. and Andrew M. Manis, eds. *Birmingham Revolutionaries: The Reverend Fred Shuttlesworth and the Alabama Christian Movement for Human Rights.* Macon, GA: Mercer University Press, 2000.

Wiesel, Elie. *Night.* New York: Hill and Wang, 1960.

Wills, Richard Wayne, Sr. *Martin Luther King, Jr. and the Image of God.* Oxford, UK: Oxford University Press, 2009.

Wilmore, Gayraud. *Black Religion and Black Radicalism.* Maryknoll, NY: Orbis Books,1989.

Williams, Reggie L. *Bonhoeffer's Black Jesus: Harlem Renaissance Theology and an Ethic of Resistance.* Waco, TX: Baylor University Press, 2014.

Wilson, William Julius. *The Bridge Over the Racial Divide: Rising Inequality and Coalition Politics.* Berkley, CA: University of California Press, 1999.

Wilson, William Julius. *The Declining Significance of Race: Blacks and Changing American Institutions.* Chicago: University of Chicago Press, 1978.

Wilson, William Julius. *Power, Racism and Privilege: Race Relations in Theoretical and Sociological Perspectives.* New York: The Free Press, 1973.

Wimberly, Anne Streety and Edward Wimberly. *Language of Hospitality: Intercultural Relations in the Household of God.* Nashville: Cokesbury, 1989.

Wink, Walter, ed. *Peace is the Way: Writings on Nonviolence from the Fellowship of Reconciliation.* Maryknoll, NY: Orbis Press, 2000.

Wiseman, Richard L. and Jolene Kesster. *Intercultural Communication Competence.* Newbury Park, CA: Sage, 1993.

Wogaman, J. Philip. *Christian Moral Judgment.* Louisville: Westminster John Knox Press, 1989.

Wogaman, J. Philip. *Christian Perspectives on Politics.* Philadelphia: Fortress Press, 1988.

Wolpert, Stanley. *Gandhi's Passion: The Life and Legacy of Mahatma Gandhi.* Oxford, UK: Oxford University Press, 2001.

Yates, Elizabeth. *Howard Thurman: Portraits of a Practical Dreamer.* New York: John Day, 1964.

Young, Josiah U. *Black and African Theologies: Siblings or Distant Cousins.* Maryknoll, NY: Orbis Books, 1990.

Young, Josiah U. *No Difference in the Fare: Dietrich Bonhoeffer and the Problem of Racism.* Grand Rapids, MI: Eerdmans, 1998.

# *Articles*

Bennet, Milton J. "A Developmental Approach to Training for Intercultural Sensitivity" in *Theories and Methods in Cross-Cultural Orientation.* Judith N. Martin, ed. International Journal of Intercultural Relations, Vol. 5, No. 2. New York: Persimmon Press, 1986.

Bennett, Milton J. "Toward Ethnorelativism: A Developmental Model of Intercultural Sensitivity" in *Cross-Cultural Orientation.* R. Michael Paige, ed. Lanham, MD: University Press of America, 1986.

Carson, Clayborne, "Martin Luther King, Jr., and the African American Social Gospel", in *African-American Religion: Interpretive Essays in History and Culture.* Timothy Fulop and Albert Raboteau, eds. New York: HarperPerennial, 1997.

Cone, James. "Theology's Great Sin: Silence in the Face of White Supremacy" in *Black Theology*, 2:2. Maryknoll, NY: Orbis Books, 2004.

Dear, John. "The Experiments of Gandhi", in *Fellowship.* New York: The Fellowship of Reconciliation, January/February, 1988.

Galilea, Segundo. "Liberation as an Encounter with Politics and Contemplation' in *The Mystical Dimension of the Christian Faith.* New York: Herder and Herder, 1974.

Gandhi, Mohandas K. "Nonviolence – The Greatest Force", in *The World Tomorrow.* New York: Fellowship of Reconciliation, October, 1926.

Gandhi, Rajmohan. "Gandhi's Unfulfilled Legacy: Prospects for Reconciliation in Racial/Ethnic

Conflict" (1995 Cynthia Wedel Lecture). Washington, DC: Church's Center for Theology and Public Policy, Wesley Theological Seminary, April 27, 1995.

Gilkes, Cheryl Townsend. "The Loves and Troubles of African American Women's Bodies", in *A Troubling in My Soul,* Emilie M. Townes, ed. Maryknoll, NY: Orbis, 1993.

Harding, Vincent. "Dangerous Spirituality", in *Sojourners Magazine.* Washington, DC: Sojourners, January-February 1999 (Vol. 28, No. 1).

Harding, Vincent. "We Must Keep Going: Martin Luther King, Jr. and the Future of America," in *Fellowship.* New York: The Fellowship of Reconciliation, January/February, 1987.

Hunt, C. Anthony. "African-American Biblical Interpretation," in *Scripture: An Ecumenical Introduction to the Bible and Its Interpretation, second edition.* Michael J. Gorman, ed. (chapter 17) Peabody, MA: Hendrickson Publishing, 2017.

Hunt, C. Anthony. "Beloved Community: Martin Luther King, Jr. and Hope for the City," in *Foundation Theology 2008,* Graduate Theological Foundation, South Bend, IN, (Faculty Publication Series, 2008).

Hunt, C. Anthony. "Beyond Afghanistan-Reflections on Peace and War", in *The United Methodist Connection,* Columbia, MD, February 2010.

Hunt, C. Anthony. "The Church and Race Relations – Then and Now (1968-2008)", in *Leading Ideas.* Washington, DC: Lewis Leadership Center, Wesley Theological Seminary, January 21, 2009. Also published in *Foundation Theology 2010,* Graduate Theological Foundation, South Bend, IN, (Faculty Publication Series, 2010).

Hunt, C. Anthony. "Easter Faith in a Good Friday World: Towards a Theology of Resurrection for the 21ˢᵗ Century African-American Church," in *Foundation Theology 2002,* Graduate Theological Foundation, South Bend, IN, 2002 (Faculty Publication Series); also in *The African Heritage Journal,* Pittsville, MD, June 2003, Vol. 9, No. 1.

Hunt, C. Anthony. "Finding Common Ground for the Common Good", in *Foundation Theology 2014,* Graduate Theological Foundation, South Bend, IN, (Foundation Publication Series, 2014).

Hunt, C. Anthony. "Giving Dangerously: Reflections on Martin Luther King, Jr.'s 'I've Been to the Mountaintop Speech'", in *The Lenten Journey.* Columbia, MD: Baltimore-Washington Conference, February 2018.

Hunt, C. Anthony. "Holding onto Hope: Reflections on the Re-election of Barack Obama", in *The United Methodist Connection,* Fulton, MD, November 2012.

Hunt, C. Anthony. "Honoring Martin Luther King's Dream: A Ten Point Plan", in *The West Virginia United Methodist,* Charleston, WV, February 2000, and in *The United Methodist Connection*, Columbia, MD, January 2001; also published by the United Methodist News Service.

Hunt, C. Anthony. "Hope Insists on a Color-blind Church" in *The United Methodist Connection,* Columbia, MD, November 2008.

Hunt, C. Anthony. "In Changing and Challenging Times – Race Still Matters", in *The United Methodist Connection,* Columbia, MD, December 2009; also in the *United Methodist Reporter.*

Hunt, C. Anthony. "The Interpretation of the Bible in African-American Churches," in *Scripture: An Ecumenical Introduction to the Bible and Its*

*Interpretation.* Michael J. Gorman, ed. Peabody, MA: Hendrickson Publishing, 2005, pp. 218-227.

Hunt, C. Anthony. "Is There a Balm? Martin Luther King, Jr., the Bible and Christian Hope", in *Foundation Theology 2006,* Graduate Theological Foundation, South Bend, IN, 2006 (Faculty Publication Series).

Hunt, C. Anthony. "I've Seen the Promised Land: The Legacy of Martin Luther King, Jr. and Prophetic Preaching', in *Foundation Theology 2016,* Graduate Theological Foundation. John H. Morgan, ed. Mishawaka, IN, (Foundation Publication Series, 2016).

Hunt, C. Anthony. "Let Us Not Forget King's Prophetic Vision", in *The United Methodist Connection,* Columbia, MD, January 2000.

Hunt, C. Anthony. "Rev. Dr. Martin Luther King, Jr. and a Letter to America", in *The United Methodist Connection,* Fulton, MD, January 2019.

Hunt, C. Anthony. "Martin Luther King, Jr. and the Quest for Beloved Community" in the *American Baptist Quarterly.* Atlanta, Georgia: American Baptist Historical Society, Spring 2018, pp. 33-51.

Hunt, C. Anthony. "Martin Luther King, Jr.'s Four Key Principles of Prophetic Witness", in *Leading Ideas,* Lewis Center for Church Leadership, Wesley Theological Seminary, January 2018.

Hunt, C. Anthony. "Redeeming the Dream: Revisiting Martin Luther King, Jr.'s Beloved Community", in *The African American Heritage Journal,* Pittsville, MD, June 2004, Vol. 10., No.1.

Hunt, C. Anthony. "Martin Luther King, Jr.: Resistance, Non-Violence and Community", in *Black Leaders and Ideologies in the South: Resistance and Nonviolence.* Preston King and Walter E. Fluker, eds. New York: Routledge, 2005, pp. 227-251.

Hunt, C. Anthony. "Martin Luther King, Jr.: Resistance, Non-Violence and Community" in *Black Leaders and Ideologies in the South: Resistance and Nonviolence.* Preston King and Walter E. Fluker, eds. London, UK: Taylor and Francis Ltd., Winter 2004, special issue - *Critical Review of International Social and Political Philosophy* , vol. 7, no.4, pp. 227-251.

Hunt, C. Anthony. "Resurrection and the African-American Church," in *Our Rising with Christ: Theological Voices from the Pastorate.* Princeton, NJ: The Center of Theological Inquiry, 2003.

Hunt, C. Anthony. "Stones of Hope: Reflections on the 50th Anniversary of the March on Washington (1950-2013)," in *The United Methodist Connection,* Fulton, MD, August 2013.

Hunt, C. Anthony. "Ten Ways to Build the Beloved Community", in *Leading Ideas,* Lewis Center for Church Leadership, Wesley Theological Seminary, January 2017.

Hunt, C. Anthony. "A Theological Framework for the Church's Role in African-American Family Preservation," *The African Heritage Theological Journal,* Ewell, MD, June 2000, Vol. 6, No. 1.

Hunt, C. Anthony. "Up Close and Personal: The Search for Peaceful Community", in *The United Methodist Connection,* Columbia, MD, January 2006.

Hunt, C. Anthony. "When Violence Abounds: A Call to Action against Violence", in *The United Methodist Connection*, Columbia, MD, March 2000.

Hunt, C. Anthony. "Where do we go from here: Chaos or Community?", in *The United Methodist Connection,* Fulton, MD, June 2018.

Hunt, C. Anthony. "Where do we go from here: Full inclusion, division or what?", in *The United Methodist Connection,* Fulton, MD, June 2017.

Hunt, C. Anthony. "A Year After – Obama and Holding onto Hope", by the General Commission on Religion and Race, The United Methodist Church, November 2009 (also by the United Methodist News Service).

Jensen, Kipton and Preston King, "Beloved Community: Martin Luther King, Howard Thurman and Josiah Royce". Atlanta: Morehouse Faculty Publication, #23, 2017.

Maguire, Mairead Corrigan. "Gandhi and the Ancient Wisdom of Nonviolence", in *Fellowship.* New York: The Fellowship of Reconciliation, June 1988.

Merton, Thomas. "Blessed are the Meek", in *Fellowship.* New York: The Fellowship of Reconciliation, May 1967.

Roberts, J. Deotis. "Gandhi and King on Conflict Resolution", in *Shalom Papers: A Journal of Theology and Public Policy,* Victoria J. Barnett, ed. *Spring* 2000, Vol. 11, No. 2. Washington, DC: Center for Theology and Public Policy, 2000.

Thurman, Howard. "Mysticism and Social Change" in *Eden Theological Seminary Bulletin IV.* St. Louis, MO: Eden Theological Seminary. (Spring, 1939).

Thurman, Howard. "The Will to Segregate", in *Fellowship.* New York: The Fellowship of Reconciliation, August, 1943.

Vertovec, Steven. "Super-diversity and Its Implications" in *Ethnic and Racial Studies* 30, no. 6 2007.

# *ABOUT THE AUTHOR*

### *C. ANTHONY HUNT, D.MIN., PH.D.*

A native of Washington D.C., Rev. Dr. C. Anthony Hunt is the Senior Pastor of Epworth Chapel United Methodist Church in Baltimore, MD, and is Professor of Systematic, Moral and Practical Theology and Permanent Dunning Distinguished Lecturer at the Ecumenical Institute of Theology, St. Mary's Seminary and University in Baltimore. He also teaches at Wesley Theological Seminary in Washington, DC, United Theological Seminary in Dayton, OH and the Graduate Theological Foundation in Oklahoma City, OK, where he is a Faculty Fellow and E. Franklin Frazier Professor of African-American Studies.

A graduate of the University of Maryland, he holds advanced degrees from Troy State University, Wesley Theological Seminary and the Graduate Theological Foundation. Additionally, he has completed post-graduate studies at the Center of Theological Inquiry, Princeton, NJ; the University of Oxford, UK; St. Mary's Seminary and University, Baltimore, MD; Bethel University, St. Paul, MN; and the Institute of Certified Professional Managers, James Madison University, Harrisonburg, Va. He is an inductee in the Rev. Dr. Martin Luther King, Jr. International Board of Preachers at Morehouse College, Atlanta, GA.

He is the author of nine other books including, *Come Go with Me: Howard Thurman and a Gospel of Radical*

*Inclusivity* (2019), *Stones of Hope: Essays, Sermons and Prayers on Religion and Race, vol. 3* (2017), and *Blessed are the Peacemakers: A Theological Analysis of the Thought of Howard Thurman and Martin Luther King, Jr.* (2005), and over 150 articles, chapters and academic papers on matters pertaining to religion and society.

www.ingramcontent.com/pod-product-compliance
Lightning Source LLC
Chambersburg PA
CBHW030820090426
42737CB00009B/808